David Busic's reputation as a gifted preacher is well established. He has now taken those gifts and applied them to the printed page. Two strong themes emerge as one reads these character sketches. First, one sees the biblical characters through the lens of their humanity—*perfectly imperfect* people. Rather than somehow diminishing the narratives, this viewpoint enhances the vibrancy and relevance of those stories for everyday twenty-first-century life. Second, one clearly sees the hand of God at work in each story in a fresh way. These portraits become a multifaceted mirror in which we see ourselves and, in doing so, find encouragement and added understanding of God's call upon our lives. Here is an engaging book for the new Christian as well as for those of us who have read these stories repeatedly.

—John C. Bowling
President
Olivet Nazarene University

According to St. Augustine, the best preaching should teach, delight, and persuade. That is exactly what David Busic offers in his new book. He teaches us much about the great "heroes" of our faith, especially about their flawed humanity. Busic then persuades us that, despite those flaws, God is pleased to use people like this (like us!) "to save [all] those who believe" (1 Cor. 1:21). And finally, throughout the book, Busic delights us with his turns of phrase, his wit and humor, but, most of all, with his profound insight into the deep and heart-wrenching truths of Scripture. You will be changed by reading this book, and you won't read the Old Testament the same.

—Brent A. Strawn
Associate Professor of Old Testament
Candler School of Theology, Emory University

D0110819

In *Perfectly Imperfect*, David Busic provides readers with reflective, creative, and practical presentations of familiar narratives and characters of the Old Testament, as well as some of the lesser-known ones. Busic's outstanding gift of communicating orally is matched by the manner in which he communicates through this text. Basing his conversational-styled presentation on solidly grounded biblical interpretation, Busic brings the narratives to life. Stories that we have heard for years take on fresh, transforming, and applicable meaning. The author masterfully fleshes out intricate literary and historical details of the texts in insightful, simple-to-understand ways. Emerging naturally from the text, the applications for day-to-day life are well grounded and practical. This book is a gift to the church and to persons of all ages, laity and clergy alike. It vividly demonstrates that even the most familiar stories of Scripture are filled with fresh and applicable meaning.

—Tim Green
Dean, Millard Reed School of Theology and Christian Ministry
Chaplain of the University
Professor, Old Testament Theology and Literature
Trevecca Nazarene University

Are you a tough audience? Just when I thought I'd heard it all, David Busic rises to the challenge of bringing fresh insights to familiar passages. Ancient texts are enlivened via humor, storytelling, and practical applications. This is transformational biblical teaching of the highest order.

—Craig Detweiler
Director, Center for Entertainment, Media, and Culture
Associate Professor of Communication
Pepperdine University

PERFECTLY IMPERFECT

CHARACTER SKETCHES FROM
THE OLD TESTAMENT

DAVID A. BUSIC

BEACON HILL PRESS
OF KANSAS CITY

ISBN 978-0-8341-3017-3

Printed in the
United States of America

Cover Design: J.R. Caines
Interior Design: Sharon Page

Library of Congress Cataloging-in-Publication Data

Busic, David A., 1964-
  Perfectly imperfect : character sketches from the Old Testament / David A. Busic.
    pages cm
  Includes bibliographical references.
  ISBN 978-0-8341-3017-3 (pbk.)
  1. Men of the Bible. 2. Character—Biblical teaching. I. Title.
  BS574.5.B87 2013
  221.9'2—dc23
                                                          2013011728

10 9 8 7 6 5 4 3 2 1

Dedicated to Christina,
the love of my life, who still makes
every day worth coming home to

CONTENTS

Foreword
9

Preface: Heroes
11

1. Everybody Gots a Father
15

2. Can You See the Water?
25

3. The Test
39

4. Red, Red Stuff
51

5. Do the Right Thing
61

6. The Glory of God
77

7. Getting Past Your Past
89

8. Mini-Me
103

9. Chasing Sardines
117

10. Beauty and the Beast
129

11. The Sound of Fine Silence
143

12. We Couldn't Stop Crying
157

13. Is Anybody Else Up There?
173

Notes
185

FOREWORD

More than twenty years ago I arrived at my first charge as lead pastor to discover, among other things, that I had inherited a youth pastor. Just a little younger than I, he rightly asked, "Do you know what to do?" I told him the truth: "No, do you?" Confessing our mutual inadequacy, we made a decision that I think fairly changed both of our lives. We decided to learn together not only what it means to shepherd a congregation but especially how to preach the Scriptures in a way that enables a fresh vision of life in the kingdom of God to be born in a people. That was a rich time for me. I learned much from my slightly younger brother that has shaped my ministry ever since.

Those days forged a friendship with David Busic that I have enjoyed these two decades and counting. Our assignments in ministry have often and happily brought us together, including the privilege of coediting *Preacher's Magazine* for several years. In my judgment there is no one in the Church of the Nazarene who more embodies the knowledge, wisdom, character, and right practices of a good pastor than does David Busic.

These reflections in *Perfectly Imperfect* are a case in point. Part of what can be discerned here for clergy and laity alike is how to do careful study of the Scriptures and then to combine that study with creative and imaginative speech so that we are brought to life-giving encounters with God through the work of the Spirit. This is partly about the skill of a good preacher, but even more than that, we see here the real and personal devotion of one who is a serious follower of Jesus Christ. And we see here the heart of a pastor who loved his people faithfully and loved them well by telling them the truth, bad as the news may be, yet he also clearly and joyfully announced the gospel.

The Bible stories may be familiar to you, but I am quite sure that Pastor Busic's telling of these episodes will draw you into them in a new way. As you are taken into the rich narratives of some of the greatest and most flawed characters of the Old Testament, you will likely begin to recognize yourself in these stories. Don't be afraid, for the essential flaws in these well-known characters of Scripture are flaws we all could find in ourselves. Yet the invitation here is to bring these flaws to a God who knows how to redeem them and by grace enable us to become "perfectly imperfect" saints.

Trust for the guide is an important part of any guided journey. David Busic is a trustworthy guide for this trip through some of the most passionate stories of the Bible. I know him very well, and there is no one in the entire world I trust more to point me toward a deeper knowledge and deeper relationship with God. It's not because David is perfect, but by the grace of God, he is *perfectly imperfect*. Enjoy the journey and may you grow "in knowledge and depth of insight" (Phil. 1:9) along the way.

—Jeren Rowell, EdD
District Superintendent
Kansas City District Church of the Nazarene
Season after Pentecost 2012

PREFACE: HEROES

Not long ago my younger daughter, Madison, was having a conversation with a good friend about what makes someone a hero. Madison said, "My hero is definitely my dad, for a lot of reasons. He is a great dad, but most of all he is my hero because he's human. He's not perfect. There were times we had our differences. But he would always come up to my room and make sure that we worked it out. Heroes become so much more real and so much greater when they are human. My dad is *perfectly imperfect*."

That phrase hit me like a ton of bricks: "perfectly imperfect." At first it sounded contradictory. How could a person be both? But the more I mull it over, the more I am convinced that it is a true and beautiful description of our life with God.

I am often struck by the blatant humanity of the heroes of our faith. They are never depicted as infallible, superhuman, or spiritual exemplars without defect. Even the best, it seems, are deeply flawed and broken people. God's Word does not try to convince us otherwise. Rather, the Bible portrays tragic accounts of imperfect people who make injurious decisions and terrible mistakes with alarming realism (Jesus seems to be the only exception).

Sometimes they recover—sometimes they don't (Lot, Samson, and Saul come to mind).

Sometimes they learn valuable lessons from their failures—sometimes they repeat the same patterns that got them in trouble in the first place (read the biographies of Abraham, Isaac, and Jacob).

The faith heroes of the Bible are frequently confused, severely tempted, and often afraid (I tried to think of some exceptions but couldn't think of any to whom this doesn't apply).

That's why these stories are not simply edifying fables with moralistic lessons at the end. They are true to life and true to faith.

Does this bother you?

Several thoughts come to mind.

First, I am thankful that the stories of our biblical faith heroes were thought important enough to be included in Holy Scripture and that they actually made the cut in all of their uncensored glory. I find it strangely comforting to know that God and, for that matter, God's people are okay with perfectly imperfect people who are in process.

The Bible does not allow any dishonesty about the human condition. We are creatures, made from dirt and dust, who need God's breath in our lungs to sustain our lives. And yet, there is a kind of glory in our humanity, because even with our imperfections we bear the image of God.

To quote one of the most perfectly imperfect people in history, we are merely "clay pots" (2 Cor. 4:7, TM), cracked just enough for the real light to shine through. That perfectly imperfect person's name was Paul, one of the first Christian leaders, who went on to say that this is exactly as it should be so that we never forget where the glory comes from.

This leads me to my second thought. Is it possible that the faith heroes of the Bible are revealed to us, not so we can emulate their virtue, but so we can learn the truth about ourselves and, more importantly, something about how God works with people like us?

Read that last line one more time.

I believe we are imperfect because we are human. But we are perfectly imperfect because God delights in taking us where we are and making us into exactly what he knows we can be. That's why it's not a crime to be perfectly imperfect. And that's why very few people in the Bible come across looking very good. But what they do end up looking like is redeemed, shot through with holiness and newness of life.

Maybe that's why, as Madison said, those people make the best heroes.

● ● ●

Here are some things you should know.

The stories collected in this book are all true. The characters are all real. No names have been changed to protect the guilty or the innocent. They are based on Old Testament stories drawn from sermons I have preached across the years at the three churches I have pastored. I am grateful to the congregations that gave me the time to wrestle with these texts and the permission to wrestle with them in the process.

It seems inadequate to say thank you to those who have made this book possible, but then again without them this book would look very different.

Thank you, Christi, for thirty years of patient, passionate, and faithful love that has allowed me to be perfectly imperfect. This book is dedicated to you. Don't forget to read what I said about you a few pages back. I tried to be poetic.

Thank you, Megan, Ben, and Madison. When I see your faces in my mind, it makes me smile. Your lives remind me that God has not given up on the world.

Thank you, Jeren, for a twenty-year friendship that continues to make me want to be a better man. Since we started the pastoral journey together, it only seems appropriate that you would write the foreword.

Thank you, Laura, for being a loyal friend with a servant's heart. You have been making my writing sound better than it is for a long time.

Thank you, Bonnie, for asking me to write . . . and asking me to write . . . and not stopping asking me to write! You made me believe not only that I had something to say but that it was something others might want to read too.

1

EVERYBODY GOTS A FATHER

GENESIS 4:1-9

God puts something good and something lovable
in every man his hands create.
–Mark Twain[1]

IN HIS DELIGHTFUL little book *Papa, My Father*, Leo Buscaglia[2]
tells the following story:

> I was observing in a classroom for mildly mentally challenged
> fourth graders. I sat beside six children and their teacher in
> their reading group. They were reading a story about a little
> duck that had no father. . . . The refrain was always: "But the
> little duck had no father."
>
> . . . When [the teacher] completed the story, she followed
> up immediately with a question-and-answer period. . . .
>
> "Martha," she asked a lovely little girl in the group, "tell
> us. Did the little duck have a father?"
>
> The child answered . . . , "Yes."

The teacher paused for a moment. . . . Finally, she smiled and said: "Martha, let me read to you again from the story. . . ."

She then repeated several parts of the story, each time accentuating the familiar refrain: "The little duck had no father."

. . . [The teacher] again asked Martha: "Did the little duck have a father?"

. . . [Martha] responded very matter-of-factly: "Yes."

The teacher's frustration was beginning to show. . . .

. . . She again read from the book: "The little duck had NO-O-O-O father." . . .

"Now," the teacher asked again sweetly, regaining her control, "did the little duck have a father?"

. . . [Martha] answered again: "Yes, the little duck had a father."

At this point the teacher totally lost control. "Martha, you disappoint me. You're simply not paying attention! It says again and again in the story that the little duck had NO father."

. . . "But, teacher," she said, "*Everybody* gots a father."

The teacher was taken aback completely. She hugged Martha in apology, smiled, and indicated that now she understood.[3]

Martha really was right. It's universal. "*Everybody* gots a father." We all know that.

We understand it biologically. We know the biological equation: a sperm + an egg = an embryo.

But we also know it spiritually. We know that *"everybody* gots a heavenly Father." A loving Father who created each of us in his own image.

And yet, in the very moment we affirm that "everybody gots a heavenly Father," we also affirm something else: biological or not, "everybody also gots a *brother.*"

● ● ●

Why does that have to be true? Why does there always have to be the "other" brother? Or to quote from the New Testament parallel, Jesus' parable of the prodigal son: Why must "a certain man" *always* have "two sons" (Luke 15:11, KJV)?

Why must there be Cain *and* Abel?

Why must there be Isaac *and* Ishmael?

Why must there be Jacob *and* Esau?

Why must there be Joseph *and* ten surly brothers?[4]

Why must there always be the "other" brother (or sister)? Couldn't we manage just fine if he (or she) wasn't around? And wouldn't life be easier without him (or her)?

I mean, let's be honest, there are disadvantages to having brothers and sisters. Having brothers and sisters means that life will never be the same for you. It means there will always be some bumps along the way that might have been smoother without them.

It means the world simply won't revolve around you anymore. You have to learn to share—to share Mom and Dad, to share the attention, to share the affection, to share the responsibility.

You even get one present from Santa Claus instead of two—all because of your brother. And then you have to share the one toy you did get with your interloping brother!

It might not be so bad, if our brothers were like us at all. But most of our brothers are very *different* from us. Those of you who are parents can attest to this. Simply being from the same womb, having the same upbringing, and living in the same house is no guarantee of a duplicate.

Just because "*everybody* gots a father," even the *same* father, there are no carbon copies. Every brother is different. Namely, he is not like you! He doesn't think like you, act like you, or even hold the same values as you.

And that makes us competitive with our brothers. So we scrawl our names in Magic Marker on *our* army men and *our* Tonka trucks and say, "Don't touch my stuff!"

When my sister and I were younger, for a short time we shared a room together. It was only a temporary arrangement, while we waited for our permanent house to be ready, but the battle lines were drawn.

We split the room in half with masking tape from the top of the ceiling, across the floor, and up the other wall. And then we threatened each other with menacing tones: "Don't cross this line. This is *my* side of the room, and I want you to stay out!" "If you even step across that line, I'm gonna knock you into kingdom come!"

Evidently, we heeded each other's warning because neither of us were ever knocked into kingdom come, and my parents seemed to be happy about that because then they would of had to come looking for us, and I don't think they knew where kingdom come was.

It reminds me of the little boy who wrote a letter to his pastor: "Dear Pastor, I would like to go to heaven someday because I know my brother won't be there."[5]

It's never easy to live with our "brothers," biologically or spiritually. Yet as much as we wish a certain God *didn't* have other children . . .

He does.

• • •

It makes you wonder sometimes, *Why does it have to be that way?*

Well, according to Martha the fourth grader, it's because "*everybody* gots a Father." And therefore, every brother and sister, regardless of how different, is cut from the same fabric. Every brother and sister shares something in common from our Father.

It's an image.[6]

You see, you carry the part of me that I am trying to recover. And every time I am with you, you are helping me to rediscover the image of God within *me*.

It's a marvelous, amazing thing, the image of God.

What is the image of God? The image of God is relationality, which is to say, all love is relational.

We do not love and cannot love in a vacuum. We need someone to be in relationship with in order to love, which means we *need* someone to love.

And because that's true, do you know what else that means? Only in relationship with my "brother and sister" can I see *myself* and *God* most clearly.

God is love. That truth is affirmed by all faith traditions, but it is foundational for Wesleyan-Holiness folks. The love of God is the lens through which we see all other attributes of the three-in-one God.

The Trinity reminds us that before there was anything else, there was a holy fellowship of perfect love. The Father loved the Son, the Son loved the Father, the Spirit loved the Son, the Father loved the Spirit, and on and on it went.

Out of this overflowing love, God created beauty, nature, order, planets, solar systems . . . and us. God didn't create us because he was lonely. God is a Trinity. God didn't create us because he needed glory. God is already glorious.

God created us because God is relational, and his love overflows into human beings so that we can share in that love. The psalm writer declares that God has crowned us with "glory and honor" (Ps. 8:5). Can this mean anything less than God has made us relational too?

So here's the logic: God places "others" in our lives, because we need *them* to help us to know *him* more personally.

It's the way we've been wired. It's the way we've been designed. It's God's image stamped on us. And therefore, the only way we can be fully what God intended us to be is in relationship with another.

I must love you in order to love God. That's where our phrase "perfect love" comes from. Love perfecting us from the *image* of God, back to the *likeness* of God.

We need the other brother.

● ● ●

This story from Genesis 4:1-9 is about the other brother.

Adam and Eve had two sons.[7] They were different—very different. One was a shepherd—the other was a farmer. One worked with flocks—the other worked in fields.

Both made offerings to God.

The text doesn't tell us why Abel's offering was received and Cain's wasn't. Why is the text silent on this? Because the issue wasn't the offering—the issue was how Cain was going to respond to his brother.

This is a story about the problem of the other brother.

Competition.

Jealousy.

Anger.

Even premeditated cold-blooded fratricide.

But here is what we cannot miss. This story is not just about the problem of the other brother, because Cain took care of that in a hurry.

It is the brother and God together that creates the conflict for Cain. Cain discovered that life with the other brother is never lived in a vacuum but always in relationship to God.

God gave Cain the opportunity to confess what was really going on. "The LORD said to Cain, 'Where is your brother Abel?'" (v. 9).

Didn't God know where Abel was?

Of course he did. God was looking for some honesty. He wanted Cain to be honest with himself, admit what had happened and why, take responsibility for his actions, and clear the way for restoration to happen.

But Cain can't give him a straight answer. "Am I my brother's keeper?" (v. 9).

"Yes, Cain, you are! That's the right answer. Despite everything you've done to try and make it otherwise, you are. This is not just about Abel. This is about our relationship too."

Cain doesn't see the connection.

One of Cain's descendants was named Lamech. Someone wounded him. Lamech takes revenge by killing him. He told his two wives, "If Cain is avenged seven times, then Lamech seventy-seven times" (v. 24).

No forgiveness. No reconciliation. No image. And the vicious cycle goes on.

When will the madness stop? Who is going to break the vicious cycle of anger, blame, retaliation, and revenge with the "other brother"?

Cain's question, "Am I my brother's keeper?" (v. 9), turns out to be answered a million times over: "Yes!"

● ● ●

Are you more loving today than you were a year ago?

Are you more compassionate? More caring? More generous? More forgiving than you were a year ago?

Are you more like Jesus?

If you can't answer those questions in the positive—and especially, if other people can't answer them in the positive about you—then you need to take a long, careful look into the nature of your walk with Christ.

Every step of progress in our spiritual life is directly related to our relationships with others. And every relationship has the potential of becoming the place of a transforming encounter with the living God.

I wish I could say that better. Isolated Christians will never experience all that God intends. It is the missing link for so many people in their journey of faith.

John Wesley said again and again that there can be no *personal* holiness without *social* holiness. But the opposite is also true. There can be no *social* holiness without *personal* holiness.[8]

Everybody gots a brother—because everybody gots a Father.

CAN YOU SEE THE WATER?

GENESIS 21:8-20

Miracles are a retelling in small letters of the very same story which is written across the whole world in letters too large for some of us to see.
–C. S. Lewis[1]

IN THE CHURCH where I grew up, Mother's Day fared pretty well for a secular holiday. It ran a close second to Easter, just nudging out Christmas and Pentecost.

The Mother's Day service always followed the same basic plan. Our pastor would have the oldest mother, the youngest mother, and the newest mother stand. It seemed a little redundant considering that our church was small enough that the oldest and youngest mothers were often the same ladies every year. Nevertheless, we would all clap for them and make them feel special for their exceptional motherhood accomplishments.

But there was one particular Mother's Day recognition that was my pastor's favorite—honoring the mother who had the most folks there because she was a mother. He loved that one. He would invite her to the front of the sanctuary and give her a gift, and then everyone would stand and applaud, while the mothers all dabbed their eyes with Kleenex.

When I was around thirteen, I can remember proposing the idea that since there was a Mother's Day, why couldn't there also be a "Teenager Day"? My mom assured me it would never fly, and besides, she said, "Corsages don't look good on teenage guys."

My memories of Mother's Day celebrations at church are all positive except for one thing: the looks on the faces of the mothers whose children were not there or of those women who did not—and some of whom will never—have children. Even as a young boy I can still remember the sadness of seeing them awkwardly trying to smile but obviously feeling a little left out and finding it difficult to hide their disappointment.

Those women's faces are the ones I see when I think about Hagar. She is the patron saint for every mother who feels left out of the Mother's Day celebrations.

To understand Hagar's situation, I need to give you a little background.

● ● ●

It all began in Genesis 12 when God called a man named Abram to leave his country, leave his home, leave his people, and go to a land God would show him.

With that call Abram was also given a promise: "I will make you into a great nation, and I will bless you; I will make your name great, and you will be a blessing. . . . and all peoples on earth will be blessed through you" (vv. 2–3).

Abram and his wife Sarai, later renamed Abraham and Sarah, obeyed and followed God. They trusted God's promise. But they also had a problem. They didn't have any children. Sarah was barren and Abraham was old. It's hard to be the father and mother of a great nation if you don't have any heirs.

They had a promise and a problem.

I read about a couple named Charan and Omkari Panwar from India. They recently set a world record for being the oldest parents in the world when Omkari gave birth to twins at the age of seventy. Charan, the proud father, was seventy-seven at the time.[2]

Abraham and Sarah were older than that. Abraham was one hundred years old and Sarah was ninety when their son Isaac was born. But even with the promise, they couldn't imagine how God could overcome the twofold problem of barrenness *and* old age.

And so they took matters into their own hands. They tried to overcome their problem by forcing God's promise.

Sarah said to Abraham, "Look, the LORD keeps saying we're going to have children, but nothing seems to be happening. However, I have an Egyptian servant girl here named Hagar. Why don't you sleep with her and see if we can have our children that way?" (16:2, author's paraphrase).

If Abraham objected to Sarah's plan, we are given no indication of it. Abraham slept with the servant girl Hagar, and she became pregnant and gave birth to a son. They named him Ishmael. Abraham was eighty-six years old when Ishmael was born. Thirteen years later Sarah became pregnant and gave birth to the promised child Isaac.

God gave them a *promise* and overcame their *problem*, but now Abraham and Sarah have created another problem. The history of the people of God makes it clear that whenever we try and force God's will to happen in the way *we* think it should happen, we always create more problems!

And the problem for Abraham is that now he has *two* sons and *two* wives, and they are competing with each other.[3]

• • •

In ancient societies the day of a child's weaning was a significant milestone and celebrated by the family with a feast for the entire community. On the day of Isaac's weaning celebration, Ishmael was acting like a junior higher, and Sarah noticed.

Maybe she saw Ishmael as a threat to Isaac's inheritance. Maybe she was just sick and tired of Abraham dividing his attention between two boys. But something had to give. Sarah puts her foot down and demands that Abraham "get rid of that slave woman and her son" (Gen. 21:10).[4]

Abraham is upset and worried about throwing them out on the street. After all, Ishmael was his own son. But after prayer, and reassurance from God, he relents, and Hagar is asked to leave.

Hagar is now a single mother, roaming around in the desert trying to survive. She is on her own, with no options and very little hope.

After a few days, bad goes to worse. Hagar runs out of water. Ishmael is beginning to die of thirst, and she cannot bear to watch. So she leaves her son under the shade of a little bush and walks away. In utter desperation she breaks down and starts to cry.

It's interesting to me that she doesn't pray. Nowhere does the text say that Hagar prayed. What it does say is that "God heard the boy crying" (v. 17).

And then "the angel of God" (which is almost always identified in the Old Testament as God himself) comes to Hagar and says: "What is the matter, Hagar? Do not be afraid; God has heard the boy crying as he lies there" (v. 17).

God hears her unarticulated prayer![5]

I love the fact that when Hagar doesn't even know what to pray, God comes to her anyway. God knows what's in her heart and loves her enough to come to her, even when she doesn't know how to come to him.

• • •

God answers her unarticulated prayer in two ways.

First, God tells her, "I know about your situation."

It's interesting that Ishmael's name literally means "God hears." And so the narrator of Genesis has given us a kind of pun on the name of Ishmael: "God has heard (divine action) God Hears (your son)."

It gives me a lot of comfort to know that God hears the cries of my children and comes to them. Even when we don't know how to reach them, or feel incapable of helping them, we serve a God who hears their cries, knows what they need, and comes to their aid.

For some moms and dads who are reading this, I want to remind you that you can trust your children to God. There have been many times that I have tried to protect my kids from potential pain and from getting hurt. And that's an appropriate thing to do when they're younger and can't fend for themselves.

But since my kids have become young adults, God often reminds me, "David, if you bail out your kids every time they have a need, then they're going to put their faith in *you* instead of *me*. And how can their faith in *me* ever deepen if they never have to depend on *me* for their help?"

Sometimes God speaks clearly enough to make me wince.

● ● ●

Ishmael is probably fourteen or fifteen years old when this story takes place. He is a teenager growing into a young man. And God wants Hagar to know that she can trust him with her son.

But notice something else: it appears God is going to save Ishmael's life through the actions of Hagar. The angel tells her, "Lift the boy up and take him by the hand [Hagar's job], for *I* will make him into a great nation [God's job]" (Gen. 21:18, emphasis added).

Do you see the divine-human partnership? God is going to do something for Hagar's son, but Hagar has to be active in her son's life for God's work to be accomplished.

This action entails a divine *and* human touch—the synergy of holy partnership.

And then . . . God opens Hagar's eyes to see a well of water.

The text says, "Then God opened her eyes and she saw a well of water. So she went and filled the skin with water and gave the boy a drink" (v. 19).

First, God answers her unarticulated prayer by coming to her family's aid. Next God answers her prayer by opening her eyes.

Now I can't prove this, but I don't think God miraculously made a water hole appear out there in the desert. I don't think he waved his magic wand, said presto, and suddenly a well miraculously appeared where there wasn't one before.

No.

I think God simply helped Hagar to look up from her grief long enough to see the provision that God had already created for her.

This is such an important point. The well had been there all the time—Hagar was just too distressed to see it.

I don't think the miracle of the story is that God created a new well of water; I think the miracle of the story is that God opened her eyes to see what was already in front of her!

That isn't to say that God isn't able to create something out of nothing. *Ex nihilo*, "out of nothing," is the story of creation.[6] God created something out of nothing. God did not build on some preexistent, eternal matter. God spoke—and there was. That certainly is in the realm of God's power. He can create something out of nothing anytime he wants to.

I was talking to a friend about his marriage. He said, "David, I don't know how to pray for my marriage. It's like we need God to do something for us we've never had. Because even at its very best, our marriage has never been what it should be. So how do I pray for God to heal our marriage if we've never had one to begin with?"

I was glad to say, "God is perfectly capable of re-creating something to be what it used to be. But our God is also perfectly adept at creating something brand new that has never been!"

I believe that! God can *renew* and *make new*. God can make something out of nothing. Abraham and Sarah having a baby together at one hundred and at ninety is proof of that.

But I don't think that's what happened here. I think God had already provided for Hagar's needs; she just couldn't see it yet.

And so the prayer of Hagar at this juncture is honestly confessing, "Lord, this isn't how I wanted things to turn out. It's not going as I had planned. But as bad as it is, I know you are with me. And so please help me to see the resources you have already provided that are right in front of me but that I just haven't spotted yet. Open my eyes, Lord!"

Open . . . my eyes.

● ● ●

What's the connection for us today?

When life gets really heavy with disappointment, grief, and sadness, sometimes the answer is not a miraculous intervention from God.

Sometimes the answer will not drop out of heaven into my lap.

Sometimes the answer is already right there in front of me, but my eyes need to be opened.

The answer is not a new life, a new wife, or a new set of circumstances. What we need is the grace to see that God has not given us a way *around* the problem but the strength to go *through* the problem.

Several years ago there was a lot of attention being given to a book called *The Prayer of Jabez*. Anybody read that book?

"[Lord,] bless me and enlarge my territory. . . . keep me from harm" (1 Chron. 4:10),[7] and all of that. We like those kinds of prayers—prayers that say, "God, I want you to do a new thing in my life. Do a *greater* thing; do a *bigger* thing."

But what about this prayer? "Lord, open my eyes to see what you've already provided but I just can't see yet."

It's probably not going to sell as many books, but my experience has been that it's a very common way for God to work.

God's answers may indeed be "on the way," and they may be something brand new and even something miraculous that God will choose to do. But it could also be that the provision of the Lord is right in front of us and that we just haven't recognized it yet.

● ● ●

You have probably heard the story about the guy caught in a terrible rainstorm. As the area he lived in began to flood, the sheriff's deputies came by and told him, "You need to leave before the river cuts off the road."

He said, "No, I'm fine. The Lord will save me."

The rain kept coming until the river was up to his front porch. Some folks came by in a boat and told him to hop in and they would take him to safety.

The guy said, "No, the Lord will save me."

The water rose above the first floor, and the man had to climb on his roof. The National Guard came by in a boat and begged the man to come with them.

"No, the Lord will save me," he told them.

The waters kept rising and the man was clinging to his chimney. A helicopter appeared and lowered a rope, but he refused to go, telling them, "The Lord will save me."

Finally, the guy drowned. He went to heaven, and he asked God, "Lord, why didn't you save me?"

God answered "I sent the sheriff, two boats, and a helicopter. What more did you want?"

Sound familiar?

The prayer of Hagar serves as a reminder not to look for the spectacular deliverance of God until we have first looked for the common provision of God.

Sometimes we want God to change the other person, when in reality everything *could* change if we would just take the first step of forgiveness.

Sometimes we want God to give us a financial miracle and relieve us from the stress of the debt we're living in, when in reality the solutions are right in front of us. It may mean hard work over a long period, but God has made a way if we'll follow it. It just looks more like spiritual discipline than it does like spiritual ecstasy.

Again, the prayer of Hagar says, "Don't look for the spectacular deliverance of God until you have looked for the common provision of God."

The prayer of Hagar says, "Don't wait around expecting God to do the extraordinary when God is perfectly willing to bless you in the ordinary."

The prayer of Hagar says, "Don't waste any time wishing for the exceptional and completely miss God's handiwork in the typical."

It's about opened eyes. It's about a graced ability to see what God has already provided for your deliverance and blessing.

• • •

I have a friend named Ronnie. When Ronnie first came to our church, he was a professional bull rider.

Ronnie soon became a Christian and wanted to serve in some way. He asked me if there was anything he could do at the church. The only thing I could think of was to ask him if he would be willing to pick up the trash in the sanctuary between morning services. I was a little hesitant to offer him the job for fear he would think it too demeaning. When I offered him the job, Ronnie said thank you with tears in his eyes. He was honored to serve God and the church in any way he could.

I watched his faith grow and his life change. Ronnie had a life-long habit of dipping snuff. All of his Wrangler jeans had a big worn ring in the back pockets. He used to sit in the front row of the church, hanging on every word I said—with a spit cup.

I was a little afraid someone in the church was going to tell Ronnie he couldn't come to church with habits like that. But nobody did.

One day Ronnie came to church without his spit cup and Skoal. I asked him about it. He said, "You know, Pastor David, it was the strangest thing. I was reading my Bible and praying the other morning, and I sensed in my heart that Jesus didn't want me to dip anymore. So I quit."

"Just like that?"

"Just like that."

"How long have you been dipping tobacco?"

"Since I was ten."

"And you just quit?"

"I don't even have the desire anymore."

I should have known that the Lord would be faithful to work in Ronnie's life. It was my job to love him; it was God's job to change him.

About six months after Ronnie became a Christian, he bought a truck. It was used, but new to him. He charged forty-five hundred dollars to his Visa. He had no insurance.

One day while he was driving down the highway, Ronnie smelled smoke. He pulled over. Before he could stop it, the truck engine had caught on fire, and in a matter of minutes the entire truck was engulfed in a ball of flames. Ronnie's new truck burned completely to the ground. It even melted all four tires.

Ronnie just sat down on the side of the road in disbelief. He was so discouraged. He didn't know what to do. He didn't have a cell phone. He just started walking home.

Ronnie noticed a piece of paper blowing down the road. For some reason he felt compelled to pick it up. There was one word written on the paper. In big, bold letters, it said, "GOD." That was it—just, "GOD."

Ronnie later told me that during the entire truck-burning epi-sode he had never even thought of God. Not a thought—not a prayer.

"But," he said, "Pastor, it was just like God to send me a little reminder, that even in the midst of my crisis he had not left me. It was like a blowing love letter from God that he was still with me."

How many times, in the middle of adversity, does God send us blowing love letters to remind us that he is still with us?

"I haven't left you. I haven't abandoned you. I'm right here."

God opened Ronnie's eyes to remind him that everything would be all right. God opened Hagar's eyes to see the water that had been there all along.

● ● ●

God loves you.

God is for you.

God knows what hurts in your life.

God knows what you are worried and anxious about.

It may seem hopeless to you now, but look up and dry your eyes. God's answer is on the way. Indeed, it may already be here!

Can you see the water?

THE TEST

GENESIS 22:1-8

Abraham, put off on your son.
Take instead the ram
Until Jesus comes.
–Sufjan Stevens[1]

WHAT DO YOU DO with a text that tells us from the very beginning that what we're about to hear is a test from God? And what do you do with a command that says, "Take your son, your only son, whom you love—Isaac . . ." (Gen. 22:2)?

Some people say Abraham was just going a little batty in his old age—you know what can happen after decades of baking in the desert sun. Others say he just misunderstood God—one bad lamb chop can make us hear funny things in the night. Some even say that Abraham was just conforming to the prevalent religious practices of his Canaanite neighbors, who often sacrificed their children to appease their unpredictable gods.

I've heard people say all kinds of things about what Abraham heard. But you can't convince me that Abraham didn't know the voice of God when he heard it. You aren't nicknamed "God's friend" (James 2:23) for nothing.

I hadn't talked to my best friend from high school in years. But when I picked up my telephone a while back, it took me all of two seconds to figure out who was calling. He said, "David?" I said, "Chris!" After all those years I still knew his voice. Why? We were best friends. How could I forget that voice?

Abraham knew God's voice. He had been walking with God now for fifty years. There had been too many things—too many conversations—too deep a friendship for him not to know God's voice. And this text won't let us decide any differently than that.

Abraham heard God's voice promise to make him a blessing. Abraham heard God's voice promise that he would inherit the land of Canaan. And most importantly, Abraham heard God's voice promise to give him a son; and against all odds, it actually happened.

It wasn't *supposed* to happen.

Let's face it—Abraham and Sarah were just flat out old.[2] Abraham was ninety-nine and Sarah was eighty-nine when God said, "This time next year, . . . Sarah your wife will have a son" (Gen. 18:10). To which the elderly couple replied, "Good one, God! That's funny!" Sarah hadn't had hot flashes in thirty years, and Abraham was old enough now that he spent most of his time pulling his pants up to his chest, complaining about the government, and watching the Weather Channel around the clock.

But just look at what God did! Suddenly Sarah's experiencing morning sickness and craving dill pickles. She's wearing maternity clothes and sleeping with a full-body pillow. Her girlfriends down at the church throw her a baby shower.

And Abraham, well, the truth of the matter is, he kind of liked going to the barbershop and having all his old checker buddies punch him in the arm and say, "You old rascal, you!"

The next thing you know, Abraham is standing in front of the labor and delivery nursery, looking through the glass with fogged up bifocals, staring at the little bundle in the bassinet. Another new father is standing next to him. He's twenty-two; Abraham's one hundred. Abraham leans over and hands him a blue bubble-gum cigar and says, "That's *my* boy!"

The whole state of affairs was so knee-slapping hilarious and totally improbable that when it came time to name him, they decided to name him *Laughter*—that is, Isaac.[3] Or as my friend Jeff says, "They called him Punch Line."[4]

God did an incredible thing! God kept his promise! You can't tell me Abraham didn't know the Voice.

Not only did Abraham know the Voice—but he knew the command as well. Because what God said to him that night were the exact words God had spoken to him fifty years before when he was in Haran: *Lekh-Lekha*.[5]

> Go forth from your country, and from your relatives and from your father's house, to the land which I will show you. (12:1, NASB)

"Go forth." Those were God's words way back in Haran, and those were the same words now. The exact same words, with one very big exception—if before God was asking him to give up his comfort and security, this time God was asking him to give up his dearest love and greatest joy.

> Take your son, your only son, whom you love—Isaac—and
> go to the region of Moriah. Sacrifice him there as a burnt
> offering. (22:2)

Burnt offering? That's not trivial. That's not minor. That's not
halfway. That's total commitment!

It was a terrifying command! Abraham loved Isaac more than he
loved himself, and now God was asking him to give him back.
Abraham had to decide how he was going to respond. How
would *you* respond?

God said, "Abraham!" (v. 1).

Abraham answered, *Hinneni!*—"Here I am" (v. 1).

Hinneni (hin-nay-nee) is a Hebrew word that literally means,
"Here, right here, right now, it's me." Here I am, willing to do
whatever you ask me to do. There is no apparent hesitation from
Abraham. There is no rebellion. Just, *Hinneni*—"Whatever you
want me to do, God—here I am, right here, right now."

Now that is not to say that the decision to obey came easy and
without anguish for Abraham. For all we know, he spent a sleep-
less night wrestling with God. But what this text wants to make
clear is that Abraham did not falter to obey the command of God.
Abraham did not shrink from obedience to God.

The reason he didn't falter is very simple.

Abraham believed that God would *do* what God had never done
before, if that's what God had to do to keep his promise.

That's worth rereading. Go ahead. I'll wait.

If God was asking Abraham to sacrifice Isaac, Abraham had faith that God could bring him back to life. The book of Hebrews tells us, "Abraham reasoned that God could even raise the dead" (Heb. 11:19).

Abraham had not seen Lazarus get up and walk away from his tomb. He hadn't seen a little girl in Capernaum raised from the dead. He didn't know that one day Jesus himself would resurrect from the dead. But he did know that God had the power to create something out of nothing. His own life was proof of that. Maybe that's why he told his two servants: "*We* will worship and then *we* will come back to you" (Gen. 22:5, emphasis added).

Abraham believed God was able to do what he had never done before if that's what God had to do to keep his promise. He may not have fully understood what God was asking him to do, but after fifty years of walking with God Abraham knew that God is dependable and trustworthy.

> Early the next morning Abraham got up and loaded his donkey. (V. 3)

Abraham didn't sit around for a week and decide if God really said what he thought he said. He instantly obeyed. His response was, *Hinneni*—"Here I am, right here, right now, ready to obey you."

Abraham was so personally vested in his response to God that he himself cut the wood for the sacrifice. Why would Abraham do that? He has dozens of servants who can cut the wood for him, two of which are right there with him. Not to mention the fact that he is now over one hundred years old. So why would he go to all that effort? Because Abraham knew that when it comes to obeying God, no one can take your place.

Abraham's small traveling band began their journey. They traveled for three days toward the region of Moriah[6] until finally Abraham saw the mountain from the distance. He told his servants to stay put while he and Isaac went on. Abraham put the wood for the burnt offering on Isaac's back, and taking the torch in one hand and the knife in the other, they began to ascend the mountain together.

● ● ●

This raises an interesting question. How old do you think Isaac was at this point? If he was a little boy, why would Abraham have a young boy carrying wood up the mountain? He probably wouldn't have.

Many Bible scholars believe Isaac was actually a teenager, or perhaps even a young man, when this episode took place. We know from Genesis 21 that Isaac has already been weaned from his mother. Hebrew children were typically weaned around the age of five.[7] Then chapter 22 begins by saying, "Some time later" (v. 1), suggesting a long period of time, probably years, has gone by.

Josephus, the great Jewish historian of the first century, estimates Isaac to be around twenty-five when this story takes place. Many scholars have closely examined the chronology of events, including the age of Sarah when she had Isaac (ninety), and her age at death (one hundred and twenty-seven), and thus estimate Isaac could even be in his early thirties at the time of this event.[8]

But in some ways it doesn't matter if he was eighteen or thirty. The point is Isaac was a full-grown man by now, not only capable of carrying a load of firewood up the mountain but also very capable of resisting a man who is now at least one hundred and twenty himself.

Would you agree?

• • •

I have a picture in my mind filled with pathos. I see an elderly man, panting and out of breath, his adult son walking beside him, holding on to his arm to keep him from falling. I see them trudging along as they inch their way up the mountain.

Can you see the scene?

As they lumber up the hill, Isaac speaks his first words of the Bible: "The fire and wood are here, . . . but where is the lamb for the burnt offering?" (Gen. 22:7). In absolute trust, Abraham answers, "God himself will provide the lamb for the burnt offering, my son" (v. 8). Abraham believes God will do whatever is necessary to keep his promise.

God . . .

will keep . . .

his promise.

Suddenly we realize that the tables have been turned. Because we thought this was mainly a test of *Abraham's* faith, but now it becomes clear that *God* is also on the line. This is not just about what Abraham is going to do—this is about what God is about to do!

> Abraham answered, "God himself will provide the lamb." (V. 8)

Father and son reach the top of the mountain, and Abraham builds an altar. Then moving very slowly, he spreads the wood across the top, while Isaac stands nearby.

Then, gently but deliberately, Abraham begins to bind his son. Do you think it's significant that there is no record of a conversation during the binding? What would you say?

There is also no record of a struggle.

If Isaac was a full-grown man, isn't it possible he could have fought off a man who was over one hundred and twenty years old? Of course he could have. And yet he doesn't. Why? This is only my musings, but perhaps deep within his heart of hearts, Isaac had come to trust in God too.

After all, Isaac had watched his father every day. He had seen his trust and his obedience. He had seen his faithfulness and unqualified surrender. And though I don't know when, I think that sometime along the way that same trust had passed on to Isaac. Though Isaac may not have fully understood what was happening in this moment, in his heart he also believed God is dependable!

Abraham binds Isaac and lays him over the wood on top of the altar. Can you imagine the heartbreaking moment when the eyes of Abraham meet the eyes of his son?

This was Abraham's dearest love and greatest joy lying on God's altar.

● ● ●

One cannot reflect on this story without asking a very important question. It may be the most important consecration question a follower of Jesus can answer.

"What is my Isaac?"

The answer can be found by answering another question: "What is the thing I love the most and am most afraid to lose?"

The question here is not what I would gladly be rid of if I had the chance. All of us would happily dispose of a sickness, a fear, or a relationship gone awry. But that's not our Isaac. Our Isaac is what has been one of God's good gifts to us. That something, or someone, that brings us the most joy and satisfaction and that we couldn't imagine living without. Our Isaac could be a child, a relationship, a career, an image, a way of life, or a dream.

I hesitate to try and qualify it more than that, because what we love the most can sometimes be so deeply entrenched in us that we even have a hard time fully understanding it ourselves. But we know what our Isaac is, because whenever it is threatened, or we are in danger of losing it, we either become

very *afraid*

or

very *angry.*

And we start trying to rein it in. We start trying to secure it and protect it. We start trying to make it happen ourselves. Bottom line?

We try to *control* it.

That's when we know what our Isaac is. It's what we try and control more than any other thing, even to the point of withholding it from God, because that would mean we would have to give up *our* control of it to *his* control.

That is always a test for us. The greatest test of our faith is not letting go of our sin, our guilt, and our pain. Who wants to hang on to those things? The greatest test of our faith is whether I can trust God with what is most dear to me. Will I even offer my Isaac completely into the hands of God?

God wants to bring us to a point in our relationship with him where we can lay our Isaac on the altar and say, "Here I am, Lord. Right here, right now. Willing to do whatever you ask me to do. Even to laying my dearest love and greatest joy before you. And not just giving it to you because I'm afraid I'll lose it if I don't. But willingly laying my Isaac down, because I want everything that is precious to me in your hands and under your control!"

Isn't that the supreme confirmation of a holy life? Everything I have on God's altar—everything I love fully surrendered to him, and under his control, including that which I love the most?

This consecrated act and his fully surrendered life is why Abraham is called the father of faith (see Rom. 4:11-16). He was all in! He held nothing back from God, not even his dearest love and greatest joy.

● ● ●

Holding nothing back, Abraham looks into the heavens and raises the knife with a shaking hand. Instantly, a voice from heaven calls out, "Abraham! Abraham!" (Gen. 22:11).[9] And once again Abraham responds, *Hinneni!*—"Yes, Lord? Here I am. I'm still listening" (see v. 11).

"Lay down the knife, Abraham." God tells him. "Now I *know* that you fear God, because you have not withheld from me your son, your only son" (v. 12, emphasis added).

Abraham looked up and saw a ram caught by its horns in the bushes. He rushes to untangle the ram and sacrifices it in Isaac's place. Not only did God see to a sacrifice, but he also gave Abraham's dearest love back—only this time, even better, because now his Isaac was fully consecrated to God.

Can you guess what Abraham called the name of that place?

The LORD Will Provide. (V. 14)

• • •

If this story sounds strangely familiar, it's because it foreshadows a much grander story. That day God the Father, God the Son, and God the Holy Spirit looked down on Abraham and Isaac and said, "We can never ask them to sacrifice what we are not willing to give first. We will see to it."[10]

And God did.

God sent his one and only Son—the Son that he loved. And his Son carried the wood for his sacrifice up a hill in Jerusalem. Jesus became the Lamb of God that willingly laid himself down and died for our sins so that we wouldn't have to.

Do you have any idea the depth of God's love for you? God took his dearest and greatest and laid down his Isaac for you. You can trust a God like that. You can surrender your life completely to a God like that.

What is your Isaac?

What do you love the most and are most afraid to lose?

Can you lay that on God's altar and say, "Here I am, Lord. Right here, right now. I am at the ready and willing to be used by you. I'm all in!"

When you do, you will discover a most amazing and humbling truth: The Lord will always provide!

RED, RED STUFF

GENESIS 25:19-34

Because of impatience we were driven out of Paradise,
because of impatience we cannot return.
—W. H. Auden[1]

YOU KNOW there is going to be conflict in a family when your twin boys are ultimate fighting in the womb. The wrestling around inside of Rebekah was so disturbing that she went to the Lord with her concern. "The LORD said to her, 'Two nations are in your womb . . . and the older will serve the younger'" (Gen. 25:23).

This was most surprising because it went against the law of primogeniture (pry-moh-jen-ih-choor), a very old and established law mandating that the oldest son should be the favored one in the family. It was the unquestioned cultural understanding in all ancient societies of how "rights" and "privileges" were to be established within families. It was the way order was maintained. And so with the prophecy "the older will serve the younger" (v. 23), there is conflict right off the bat.

Shortly thereafter, the twin boys are born. The first one to come out was bright red and covered with hair. So it made sense to call him Red Hairy Guy. Not Harry, as in Harry Truman or Harry Potter. But Hairy, like Ted Nugent or Chewbacca. However, because the name Red Hairy Guy didn't exactly roll off the tongue, they decided to go with Esau instead.[2]

Within seconds of Esau being born, his brother came out doing a very odd thing. He was actually hanging on to the back of his brother's foot, grasping on to his heel, almost as if they were competing to see who would be the firstborn. So his parents decided to call this boy Jacob, which means the "heel-grabber," the "one who grasps and deceives." As odd as it may seem, those were their names: Hairy and Heel-Grabber—Esau and Jacob.[3]

Now I don't know if the names made the boys or if the boys made the names, but I do know these two fellows were not promising candidates to be the ancestors of Jesus.

As they grew up, their personalities emerged. Though they were twins, the boys could not have been more different. Esau was a strapping, strong, charismatic, follicly well-endowed man's man who wore flannel shirts, drank Red Bull, and drove a Ford F-150 with a gun rack. He was a skilled hunter who knew how to live off the land and could survive for days in the open country. But he was also loud, boisterous, and full of himself (think Gaston in *Beauty and the Beast*).

Jacob was a little smaller, smooth-skinned, and more sensitive. He was a brainy guy who wore polo shirts and pleats in his pants, watched the Cooking Channel, sipped lattes at Starbucks, and drove a Volvo. He was generally kind of a momma's boy who stayed close to home and focused on domestic matters.

They were absolute and complete opposites. They were just so different that you knew there were going to be problems.

But if that wasn't troublesome enough, their parents didn't help the situation. They clearly played favorites with their boys. Isaac, the dad, loved Esau more than Jacob. And you can understand why he might do that. Esau liked to hunt. He was confident. He played sports. He was a winner. And most importantly, Esau was Isaac's firstborn son—all the things that Jacob was not. And so Isaac doted on Esau.

Meanwhile, Rebekah, the mom, loved Jacob more than Esau. Jacob helped around the house. He did some of the cooking. He was obviously smarter than his brother. What Esau had in brawn, Jacob had in brains. He could carry on an intelligent conversation. He cared about the same things Rebekah cared about.

Her mother's intuition also told her Jacob was an insecure kid, with a major family disadvantage, and so she became very protective of him. In fact, as the story goes on, and you read between the lines, you begin to wonder if she even liked Esau. She was willing to do whatever it took to see Jacob succeed and Esau fail.

As a result of their parents' flagrant favoritism, emotional devastation is unleashed on both boys, and their characters are ravaged by the preferential treatment. Esau grew up to be willful and proud, with no self-control. Jacob turned into a liar and schemer with no self-esteem; he desperately wanted to be loved and accepted by his father and was willing do anything to gain his father's approval, even if it meant cheating.[4]

● ● ●

We pick up the story when the brothers are both young adults. Esau has been out on a hunting trip. He's been gone all day and completely struck out. Not only does he not bring home any game, but he hasn't eaten either. He thinks he's starving!

Meanwhile, Jacob is doing what he does best—cooking something up. He is making a stew of some sort. Esau comes in downwind and can smell the food from a mile away. And so when he gets into camp, Esau says to Jacob (and I am quoting exactly the way the Hebrew language says it in the text): "Quick! Give me a gulp of that red, red stuff; that red stuff there!"[5] (Gen. 25:30).

Robert Alter, one of the world's greatest scholars of ancient Hebrew, says it's almost as if the narrator is trying to tell us how completely dense Esau is in this moment. It's as though he is speaking some kind of substandard Hebrew from the first grade.[6]

Esau repeats the word "red" three times for emphasis. He is so out of his mind with hunger that he can't even come up with the ordinary Hebrew word for stew or soup. Instead, all he can do is point to the bubbling pot in front of him and say, "Quick! Give me a gulp of that red, red stuff; that red stuff there!"[7]

The word here for "gulp" occurs nowhere else in the Bible, but in rabbinic writings it refers to the feeding of animals. Can you picture your dog eating a piece of meat? So what does this mean? Very simply, at this moment Esau is unbelievably crude and completely blinded by his appetite.

If Esau is crude, Jacob is calculating.

Jacob says, "Let's make a deal. You sell me your birthright and I'll give you a bowl of stew" (see v. 31).

You may not be laughing right now, but that is really funny. Because the difference between a birthright and a bowl of stew is so disproportionate!

That would be like saying, "I'll trade you my 1927 Babe Ruth vintage condition baseball card for your Pee-wee Herman Wonder Bread card."

Or "You give me your brand-new Callaway golf clubs, and I'll give you this hamburger."

Ludicrous!

It's the same thing here. Jacob wants to trade a bowl of that red stew for Esau's birthright? How could he possibly think that Esau would be dumb enough to fall for that?

● ● ●

The birthright was an incredibly valuable asset for a person to have. It was the equivalent of being in the driver's seat of your family. It made you the primary leader in your clan and placed you in the privileged position of status in your community. It was extraordinarily valuable and important.

Jacob is asking Esau if he wants to sell *that* for a couple of gulps of soup? Do you see what a crazy proposition that is?

But that is exactly how off-kilter Esau has become. He is so focused on his immediate appetite that he can't see the long-term implications. The ever eloquent Frederick Buechner wrote, "He was [so] ravenously hungry after a long day in the fields—his birthright look[ed] pale and intangible beside the fragrant reality of a good meal."[8]

He traded his birthright for beans.

● ● ●

Rhett Bomar was the number one rated high school quarterback in the nation when he enrolled at the University of Oklahoma

(OU) in 2004. He became the starting quarterback of the Sooners the second game of his redshirt freshman year.

He was a rare talent. He was very fast, with a rocket arm. He had a high IQ (at least football smart) and was a good-looking kid. And he had a very cool name for a football player—Rhett Bomar! By the end of the year, he was the MVP in the Holiday Bowl against Oregon.

He was nineteen years old.

Rhett Bomar had everything going his way. He could have been OU's quarterback for four years, broken every passing record at the school, possibly won the Heisman Trophy, had a career in the NFL, and then returned to be governor of Oklahoma. He could have done all that.

But he didn't.

Do you know what he did instead? He traded his birthright for a bowl of "red, red stuff."

He violated NCAA rules by taking some money from a booster who owned a car dealership. He was busted, kicked off the team, and lost everything he might have had. And for what? For a few thousand dollars.

He threw it all way for some "red, red stuff."

I'm not trying to pick on Rhett Bomar. He was just a kid that got caught up in more hype than he was prepared for. I feel for him. I hope he gets a second chance. None of us want to be judged for the rest of our lives by something we did when we were nineteen.

But that kind of thing happens all the time. People trade infinitely precious things *that should never be for sale* for infinitely less important things, because they think they have to have it now.

They trade their birthright for beans.

● ● ●

Notice the two words that the storyteller associates with Esau: "quick" and "gulp." That is the epitome of instant gratification. That is the essence of living according to the flesh. "I want to satisfy my appetites now, even if it means selling out something vastly more important for later."

When the text says, "Esau despised his birthright" (Gen. 25:34), it didn't mean he hated it or wanted to be rid of it. It meant he didn't understand its ultimate value.

He cheapened it.

He didn't want to lose his birthright! He just couldn't see what it could do for him in that moment. He took something of inherently great value and traded it for something of far less value in the moment.

Bottom line: he was hungry and he wouldn't wait.

That's how addictions begin.

That's how bad relationships get started.

That's how compromises are made.

That's how health gets broken.

That's how integrity is lost.

That's how reputations are tarnished.

People who want instant gratification over deferred blessing. People who are hungry and choose not to wait.

That was Esau.

● ● ●

What about Jacob?

Jacob knew Esau's weakness and took advantage of it. He knew his brother was shallow and impetuous. He knew he was used to getting what he wanted. He knew he could be bought.

But does Jacob win brownie points because he's more shrewd and opportunistic than his dense brother? No. He was chasing after his own "red, red stuff."

Jacob was just as self-seeking and just as much living according to the flesh as Esau was. He didn't feel loved by his father and was so desperate to find approval in his life that he was willing to sell his twin brother down the river just to have a taste of it.

Esau may have despised his birthright, but Jacob despised his brother.

That struggle never really goes away for Jacob. There will be constant conflict in Jacob's life. He fights with his brother, with his dad, with his wives, and with his father-in-law, and ultimately Jacob persists in a huge ongoing dispute with God over who will be in supreme control of his life.

It's as if Jacob is born into a kind of restlessness that makes him a grasper, conning every person and exploiting every situation. And as a result of his hurt and insecurity, he ends up hurting all the people around him as well.

It's not an uncommon problem.

• • •

This is not an edifying story with a positive moral lesson at the end. This is not intended to be a story of examples to follow. Jacob and Esau were both wrong—dead wrong! Neither one is a hero—neither one is a spiritual giant.

And neither is Isaac, neither is Rebekah, nor any one of the rest of this entire messed up family.

Which makes me wonder why God stuck with these people?

I mean, why didn't God decide to get rid of the whole sorry bunch and start over? Surely God could have done a whole lot better than this. Surely God could have found some more credible people, who had their act together to be the ancestors of Jesus.

But he didn't.

And maybe that's the point of the whole Jacob and Esau story: God chooses to work with very weak and deeply flawed people.

God didn't cause this conflict between the brothers. The prophetic word to Rebekah was about what *would* be, not what *had* to be. They made bad decisions that had serious consequences. But God bound himself to this family, and he would not let them go.

And that's another lesson learned from this story: God does not run from us when we blow it.

God doesn't take off when he sees the trouble we're in or the trouble we've caused. He stays with us. He never leaves us. Sometimes God works in *spite* of us, but he always works *with* us. He doesn't run from our trouble; he runs toward us.

I'm sad to report this, but as far as I can tell, Jacob never initiates a conversation with God. Not once. But God relentlessly keeps showing up in Jacob's broken and messed up life to help, redirect, and redeem.

That's why Jesus came to earth: to bring peace to our mess, to make sense of our confusion, to redeem our bad decisions, to forgive us of our sins, and to make us like himself. And he never gives up on his purpose or on us.

That ought to be good news for those who feel that everywhere they turn, there is nothing but trouble and struggle.

Our troubles do not repel God; they draw him to us. They are opportunities for us to come face-to-face with the living God and to be reminded that he is bound to us and will not let us go.

That's God's job. Our job is to stop chasing "red stuff."

5

DO THE RIGHT THING

GENESIS 40-41

Righteousness is easy in retrospect.
–Arthur Schlesinger Jr.[1]

GENESIS 40 begins with three informative words: "Some time later" (v. 1). Apparently, Joseph has been in prison for some period.

It has been eleven years since he was first sold into slavery by his brothers. He was seventeen then, and he will be thirty when he is released from prison. We don't know how long he was in Potiphar's house, but assuming that was five or six years, we could say that Joseph has now been in prison for at least three years.

We are also introduced to two more characters in the story. They are officials in Pharaoh's royal court, cabinet members in his administration. These are well-to-do guys with what appear to be pretty cushy jobs.

One was Pharaoh's baker. He was in charge of ensuring that the king had an ample supply of cupcakes, bran muffins, and pecan pie. Not a bad job on the surface, but as we'll find in a moment, it had the potential of some bad side effects.

The other was Pharaoh's cupbearer. It was his job to ensure that the king had the best wine possible. So he would sample all the wine for quality control and then give it a thumbs-up or thumbs-down. But this was also a job that required its holder to be a loyal and trustworthy person, because he also checked the wine to be sure it was safe and that no one had poisoned it. There was only one way to find that out. The cupbearer took a couple of drinks of it first, and if he didn't get thrown into convulsions and die, then he would pour a glass for the king. Kind of a dangerous job really.

It appears both the cupbearer and baker had hazardous jobs. Normally you wouldn't think about baking cookies and wine tasting as being all that perilous. But in their line of work, if you made the king mad for any reason, you didn't just get fired; you served time, or worse.

Somehow these two managed to offend Pharaoh. I don't know what they did. Maybe the baker was trying to get him on a low-carb diet or the cupbearer tried to slip him some wine in a plastic bottle from 7-Eleven. "No cookies? Cheap wine? You're both going to jail!"

At any rate, they're thrown into prison and by a strange "coincidence" end up in the same place as Joseph. Coincidence for the Christian, of course, is code for God undercover.

You may remember that Joseph has already been put in charge of the prison (see 39:22).[2] The steward of the jail assigns Joseph to specifically take care of the cupbearer and the baker while they await their final sentencing. Again, the narrator wants us to know that this was also God working behind the scenes, putting Joseph one step closer to the king.

While they are in jail, the cupbearer and the baker both have a dream on the same night. Maybe they were having breakfast together the next morning. One says to the other, "I had the weirdest dream last night." The other one says, "No kidding! Me too!" And they start talking about their dreams, and it messes with them because they know the dreams mean something.

Sometimes people have bad dreams because of too much chili. But sometimes people have dreams that are significant. The cupbearer and the baker both knew these dreams had a special meaning, and it bothered them.

Joseph walked in and could see by the looks on their faces that they were upset. So he asked them about it. They told him that they both had dreams and that they didn't have anyone to interpret them.

In Ancient Egypt, the interpretation of dreams was regarded as a science, and formal instruction in interpretation techniques was given in schools called "houses of life."[3]

The cupbearer and the baker are looking for a professional dream interpreter, but Joseph makes a very important theological assessment. Since God can give people dreams, he can also reveal their meaning if a person is really listening. Joseph says, "I am such a person. Tell me the dreams."

Here is the account.

> So the chief cupbearer told Joseph his dream. He said to him, "In my dream I saw a vine in front of me, and on the vine

were three branches. As soon as it budded, it blossomed, and its clusters ripened into grapes. Pharaoh's cup was in my hand, and I took the grapes, squeezed them into Pharaoh's cup and put the cup in his hand."

"This is what it means," Joseph said to him. "The three branches are three days. Within three days Pharaoh will lift up your head and restore you to your position, and you will put Pharaoh's cup in his hand, just as you used to do when you were his cupbearer." (40:9-13)

"Pharaoh will lift up your head" (v. 13). That's a good thing. To "lift up your head" means restoring someone to a place of honor and respect. The inability to "raise your head" is synonymous with indignity, shame, and a state of subjection. So Joseph says, "In three days you will regain your dignity and your honor."

Joseph continues: "But when all goes well with you, remember me and show me kindness; mention me to Pharaoh and get me out of this prison. I was forcibly carried off from the land of the Hebrews, and even here I have done nothing to deserve being put in a dungeon" (vv. 14-15).

The cupbearer was obviously relieved. The chief baker was hopeful too. He heard good news for the cupbearer, and he wanted some good news as well.

When the chief baker saw that Joseph had given a favorable interpretation, he said to Joseph, "I too had a dream: On my head were three baskets of bread. In the top basket were all kinds of baked goods for Pharaoh, but the birds were eating them out of the basket on my head."

"This is what it means," Joseph said. "The three baskets are three days. Within three days Pharaoh will lift off your head and impale your body on a pole. And the birds will eat away your flesh." (Vv. 16-19)

Pharaoh will not "lift *up* your head"; he will "lift *off* your head" (vv. 13, 19, emphasis added). That's not a positive interpretation. Moreover, executions in Egypt meant not only getting your head cut off but also having your corpse publicly exposed by being impaled on a spiked pole in the ground. It was a double form of dishonor, especially considering the Egyptian spiritual beliefs about the afterlife that required preserving the body (hence the pyramids). It was bad enough to die, but then to lose out on the afterlife was a real bummer.

Can you imagine how awkward the next three days were around the jail?

"Hey, Cookie. How's it going?"

"Well, not so good, Joe. Considering I've got forty-eight hours until my decapitation."

Here's what happened next.

> Now the third day was Pharaoh's birthday, and he gave a feast for all his officials. He lifted up the heads of the chief cup-bearer and the chief baker in the presence of his officials: He restored the chief cupbearer to his position, so that he once again put the cup into Pharaoh's hand—but he impaled the chief baker, just as Joseph had said to them in his interpretation. (Vv. 20-22)

As a sidenote, how foul-tempered do you have to be to *execute* a guy on your birthday? Especially when it's the guy who just baked your birthday cake!

The chief cupbearer, however, did not remember Joseph; he forgot him. (V. 23)

Before we go any further, I want you to stop and think for a minute. One of the difficult things about the Joseph story is that we can't take it seriously. I don't mean we can't take it seriously as far as whether or not it's true. I mean we can't take the *plot* seriously, because we know how the story ends.

It's like watching a movie for a second time or a football game when you already know the final score. You still enjoy watching, but the suspense isn't quite at the same level. Why? Because you know how it's all going to end.

Most of us are so familiar with Joseph's story, and how it all turns out for his good, that we forget that is not where he is right now.

Joseph reached out in compassion and tried to help some friends. He tried to bring honor to God by giving him the credit for the interpretation of the dreams. He did the right thing!

But where did that get him? He's still behind bars, he's still wearing rags, he's still sleeping on the floor, he still can't get a bath, and he's still paying the price of being framed by Potiphar's wife.

We know the end of Joseph's story. But he didn't.

And for now, he feels forgotten.

● ● ●

Life is like that sometimes. There is often a delay between the promise of God and the fulfillment of that promise.

Abraham had to wait twenty-five years before Isaac was born. Jacob waited fifteen years before he could return home. Moses spent decades in the wilderness before God called him to go back to Egypt. For all of these, and others, I'm sure it seemed like a long time to wait for God's promise to be fulfilled.

But it didn't mean that God wasn't working on their behalf. He was preparing them for their destiny. He was making them into the persons he wanted them to be. He was teaching them patience. He was performing heart surgery so that they would depend on him and not on their own strength or abilities.

That's the way it often is for us.

We "live," as Walter Brueggemann says, "bracketed between the *hint of the dream* and the *doxology of the disclosure*."[4] We live between the promise and the fulfillment—between what *is* and what we pray *will* be. God seldom works on our timetable, and none of us like to wait.

But here's the thing about providence: if you have a God great enough and transcendent enough to be mad at because he hasn't intervened in the way you thought he should, then at the same moment, you must also have a God great enough and transcendent enough to have good reasons that you can't possibly know or understand for allowing a situation to continue.[5]

We can't have it both ways.

God seldom works on our timetable, and we often have to wait, but it doesn't mean God isn't working. He is doing his work and preparing us for his larger plan.

And so for now, Joseph will have to wait.

For two more years.

● ● ●

Two years went by—two years.

And then something extraordinary happened. Pharaoh had a dream.

> When two full years had passed, Pharaoh had a dream: He was standing by the Nile, when out of the river there came up seven cows, sleek and fat, and they grazed among the reeds. (Gen. 41:1-2)

That particular grazing activity wasn't unusual in Egypt. The cows would often go down into the river Nile and nearly submerge themselves in the water to escape the heat and the flies.

This is where it starts to turn into a Tim Burton movie.

> After them, seven other cows, ugly and gaunt, came up out of the Nile and stood beside those on the riverbank. And the cows that were ugly and gaunt ate up the seven sleek, fat cows. Then Pharaoh woke up. (Vv. 3-4)

Yes, you read that correctly. Now there are seven ugly, skinny cows that turn into carnivores.

Pharaoh had another dream.

> He fell asleep again and had a second dream: Seven heads of grain, healthy and good, were growing on a single stalk. After them, seven other heads of grain sprouted—thin and scorched by the east wind. The thin heads of grain swallowed up the seven healthy, full heads. Then Pharaoh woke up; it had been a dream. (Vv. 5-7)

When Pharaoh woke up the next morning, he was very upset. So he did what all Pharaohs do in times like that—he called a staff meeting.

In the morning his mind was troubled, so he sent for all the magicians and wise men of Egypt. Pharaoh told them his dreams, but no one could interpret them for him. (V. 8)

Ancient Israelites believed dreams were a means by which God could speak to humans, but they did not believe in magic or sorcery. Egyptians, on the other hand, did believe in magic and even developed a special class of magicians. I don't mean "pulling rabbits out of hats" and "card trick" magicians. These were professional sorcerers who would attempt to divine meaning from the spirit world. So the first people Pharaoh went to with his dreams were the magicians.

Pharaoh brought in the whole bunch of them, but no one could interpret the dreams for him. It's not because they weren't trying. Don't you think that the "dream team" was trying? You better have some really good insights if Pharaoh calls you in.

I'm sure they had plenty of theories. But all of their interpretations were merely attempts to impress him with flattery and good news, and he wasn't buying it.

As an aside, these dreams were different from all of the previous dreams in Genesis. In each of the earlier dreams, the dreamer played a central role in the meaning of the dream. But there was nothing personal about Pharaoh's dreams, and it was clear to him that his dreams had a wider, more national significance.

Everyone was stumped. What were they going to do?

Then the chief cupbearer said to Pharaoh, "Today I am reminded of my shortcomings. Pharaoh was once angry with his servants, and he imprisoned me and the chief baker in the house of the captain of the guard. Each of us had a dream the same night, and each dream had a meaning of its own. Now a young Hebrew was there with us, a servant of the captain of the guard. We told him our dreams, and he interpreted them for us, giving each man the interpretation of his dream. And things turned out exactly as he interpreted them to us: I was restored to my position, and the other man was impaled."

So Pharaoh sent for Joseph, and he was quickly brought from the dungeon. When he had shaved and changed his clothes, he came before Pharaoh. (Vv. 9-14)

It had been a long time since Joseph had seen the light of day. He hadn't had a shave or a bath in a couple of years, and you couldn't meet the king in rags.

Joseph prepared to meet the most powerful man in the entire world.

Pharaoh said to Joseph, "I had a dream, and no one can interpret it. But I have heard it said of you that when you hear a dream you can interpret it." (V. 15)

This was an incredibly important moment for Joseph. You could say his future, if not his very life, hung in the balance. What would you say?

I love Joseph's humility.

"I cannot do it," Joseph replied to Pharaoh, "but God will give Pharaoh the answer he desires." (V. 16)

Let's remind ourselves who Pharaoh was.

Pharaoh was the ruler of the most dominant superpower on earth. Egypt would maintain that ranking for thirteen hundred years.[6]

To this day, it still holds the distinction of being the most prolific empire in the history of the world.

But pharaohs were more than rulers—they were gods, chosen to lead the people, maintain order, and be go-betweens for the Egyptian people and the other gods.

The Pharaohs were considered divine. And make no mistake, Joseph knew their theology. He knew that Pharaoh considered himself a god! Nevertheless, Joseph made a bold declaration: "God will give Pharaoh the answer he desires" (v. 16). In other words, there is a God and you aren't him.

Most of us wouldn't have the courage to do that, much less to say, "I can't help you."

Imagine you had been in prison for a couple of years and the president of the United States called you into the Oval Office to ask for your help, with the promise of a pardon if you succeeded. You would be talking fast and making stuff up on the spot!

President: "Can you help us be the first country to put a person on Mars?"

You: "Absolutely! I've been working on that plan for years!"

Joseph knew that Pharaoh had the power to set him free. But he kept the focus on God. And amazingly, Pharaoh shared his dreams with Joseph.

After he had heard the dreams, Joseph gave Pharaoh their meaning. He told Pharaoh that the dreams were actually one and the same. The cows represented years—seven years of prosperity and seven years of famine. The fact that there were two dreams with one meaning was verification that it was going to happen and happen soon.

Then Joseph made a recommendation. "You need to select a smart leader to form and execute a strategic plan, appoint some regional overseers, and organize a grain storage system."

It made a lot of sense to Pharaoh and his officials. So Pharaoh asked the next logical question: "Can we find anyone like this man, one in whom is the spirit of God?" (v. 38).

It is a rhetorical question. No answer is required. Everybody knows what Pharaoh is about to do—because Joseph is the only person in the entire country who has the Spirit of God in him. And Pharaoh can see it.

The next time these words are used to describe someone was hundreds of years later referring to a young man named Daniel. This is not just a story about dreams or interpretations. This is about God putting his Spirit in a man named Joseph and leading him to save thousands of lives, including the nation of Israel.

> Then Pharaoh said to Joseph, "Since God has made all this known to you, there is no one so discerning and wise as you. You shall be in charge of my palace, and all my people are to submit to your orders. Only with respect to the throne will I be greater than you." (Vv. 39-40)

Wasn't Joseph an inmate just a few hours before?

> Pharaoh said to Joseph, "I hereby put you in charge of the whole land of Egypt." (V. 41)

Joseph is now the prime minister.

Then Pharaoh took his signet ring from his finger and put it on Joseph's finger. (V. 42)

The signet ring represented all the authority of Pharaoh himself.

He dressed him in robes of fine linen and put a gold chain around his neck. (V. 42)[7]

Joseph trades his prison stripes suit for an Armani suit.

He had him ride in a chariot as his second-in-command, and people shouted before him, "Make way!" (V. 43)

Joseph was given both power and status. The Hebrew phrase "make way" means "bend your knee."

Thus he put him in charge of the whole land of Egypt. (V. 43)

From prisoner to prime minister! From slave to CEO of the whole country!

Joseph was thirty years old when he left prison to run an empire. Pharaoh gave Joseph his complete trust. The land prospered in astounding ways during the years of abundance. The accountants stopped counting the profit.

When the years of famine came, Egypt was positioned and prepared. The famine was so severe that it impacted the world economy. Nations from around the world came to Egypt for aid. Because of this, Egypt continued to prosper, even during a global economic collapse.

• • •

Joseph must have been quite a person.

Everywhere he goes, he seems to rise to the top: in his father's house, in Potiphar's house, in an Egyptian prison, in Pharaoh's court, and in Egypt's government.

Why?

Is it because of his Brad-Pittish good looks? Is it because of his immense charm? Is it because of his managerial skills? Is it because of his unusual charisma?

No.

It is because no matter what happens, Joseph keeps doing the right thing. And because Joseph keeps doing the right thing, God knows he can trust him.

Because of the Lord's favor on Joseph, not only is Joseph successful in all that he puts his hand to, but he also can rise up again and again in circumstances that would crush most people.

What if Joseph had given up?

What if he had become bitter and stopped doing the right thing? What would have changed? Would thousands of lives have been saved? Would his family have starved to death? What would have happened?

Joseph didn't know the purpose of his slavery. He didn't know prison would become a platform to one day rule over Egypt. He didn't know any of that. He just did what he knew was right in the moment and trusted God with his future.

• • •

What do we learn from this story?

Even when it doesn't look as if doing the right thing will get you *what you want*, doing the right thing will always get you *where you need to be*.

Knowledge is not wisdom, and wisdom is not virtue. Knowledge is knowing what to do. Wisdom is knowing what to do next. Virtue is doing it.[8]

My friend J. C. Watts says it this way: "Character is doing the right thing when nobody's looking. There are too many people who think that the only thing that's right is to get by, and the only thing that's wrong is to get caught."[9]

What's right or wrong isn't based on what I can get away with. Very often doing the right thing will be the hardest choice to make, with great personal risk in the moment.

Some people will say, "I tried to do the right thing for a long time, and it didn't work."

Your story isn't finished yet. God is still working. Just keep doing the right thing.

When you're tempted to cut corners and compromise because it feels as if you aren't getting anywhere—keep doing the right thing.

When you lose the promotion at work because you won't go party with the rest of the office—keep doing the right thing.

When you lose some extra income because you refuse to cheat your customers—keep doing the right thing.

When your boyfriend breaks up with you because you won't have sex with him—keep doing the right thing.

When you kick your drug habit and your life seems to just get harder—keep doing the right thing.

When you are following God and you still get sick—keep doing the right thing.

Even when you think no one knows what you're doing and that you've been completely forgotten—just keep doing the right thing.

Remember this: even if you get what you want by doing it the wrong way, God will never bless that, and there will be no joy or satisfaction in it in the end.

God can use those who are willing to do the right thing no matter what. God can put people in positions of authority and influence as he chooses, but it will never be simply for personal power and prestige. He will put you there to be a blessing to the world and to honor his name.

No matter what chapter your story is in, God has a few more lines he'd like to write.

So keep doing the right thing, and God will vindicate you and work through you to save lives and bring him glory.

THE GLORY OF GOD

EXODUS 33:1-11

You never have to advertise a fire. Everyone comes
running when there's a fire. Likewise, if your church
is on fire, you will not have to advertise it.
The community will already know it.
–Leonard Ravenhill[1]

The year of grace 1654 … From about half past ten
at night until about half past midnight, FIRE.
–Blaise Pascal[2]

MOSES and the children of Israel have been rescued from the tyr-
anny of the Egyptians by the hand of God. Now they are on their
way to the Promised Land. But then God says a surprising thing
to Moses: "I will not go with you, because you are a stiff-necked
people and I might destroy you on the way" (Exod. 33:3).

To understand that statement we must go back to an event that
happened in Exodus 32. It's a very famous episode in which God
leads the people to Mount Sinai (or what is sometimes called
Mount Horeb).

Moses tells the people to wait at the base of the mountain until he comes back, and then he climbs the mountain to receive the law of God, which is the covenant guideline by which the people are called to live.

Clouds and darkness and thunder and lightning descend on that mountain. And for weeks upon weeks the people of Israel dwell in the shadow of this mountain that is burning, smoking, and trembling with the power of God.

Meanwhile, Moses doesn't come back for a long, long time. The people begin to get confused and afraid until finally they approach Aaron, the brother of Moses who was second in command, and pressure him to give them a new god.

And so Aaron collects all the gold earrings and other jewelry from the people and casts them into a golden calf that the people begin to worship. They offer sacrifices to it, bow down to it, dance around it, and just generally carry on like crazy people.

Now obviously, God knows what's going on, and so "the LORD said to Moses, 'Go down, because your people, whom you brought up out of Egypt, have become corrupt. They have been quick to turn away . . .'" (32:7-8).

This is one of the most famous examples of spiritual backsliding in the history of the people of God, because here is a group of people who have just seen God do great and amazing things: he has redeemed them from captivity in Egypt, he has parted the waters of the Red Sea, he has led them through the desert, he has given them manna and quail to eat, and he has provided them with water from a rock to drink.

And yet, "they have been quick to turn away" (v. 8).

To "turn away" in this context means that they have rejected the living God to worship lifeless idols. They have gone from being spiritually hot to freezing cold.

You might be saying, "I don't get it. How could anyone forget about the plagues in Egypt and the Red Sea? I mean, I just saw it in a movie with Charlton Heston, and I can't get it out of my mind. I can't imagine turning away if it had actually happened to me."

But here's the truth of this story: no matter how strong your experience of God may be, no matter how close you think you've gotten to him, no matter how spiritually hot you are—if you don't tend your spiritual fire, you will cool off and grow cold.

● ● ●

I am a city boy, born and raised. I am used to setting a thermostat to the room temperature I want and just leaving it alone. I know it won't fluctuate more than a degree or two from the setting I select. A campfire, however, is very different from that. No matter how hot a campfire may be, if it is not tended, it will eventually go out. The embers of a campfire must be stoked and stirred to remain hot.

Some people think their spiritual life is like a thermostat. They set it at a particular temperature once or twice a year and then don't pay much attention to it in between. But our spiritual lives are the exact opposite. Spiritual fires that are not given much attention will die down and eventually die out.

This is why every Christian needs fresh infillings of the Holy Spirit.[3] Recognizing this need is why my own tradition (the Church of the Nazarene) puts so much emphasis on revivals and focused times set aside for spiritual renewal.

If you don't tend your spiritual fire, you will cool off and grow cold.

• • •

The LORD said to Moses, . . . "I will not go with you." (Exod. 33:1, 3)

When the Israelites heard what God had said to Moses, they were distraught. They knew they had grieved God, and the very thought of it grieved their hearts too. They wanted to repent but weren't sure how.

God said, "Now take off your ornaments and I will decide what to do with you" (v. 5).

What an odd thing to command. What are ornaments and why does God want them taken off?

An ornament is something used for decoration. Christmas ornaments are decorations on trees. Hood ornaments are decorations on cars. Musical ornaments are flourishes in a composition to decorate a song.

Ornamentation in the Scriptures refers to fancy clothes and jewelry. Just like our society today, people would ornament themselves for special occasions and festivals. God said, "Take off your ornaments" (v. 5).

Is God against jewelry? Is that what this command is about?

Taking off our ornaments in this context could mean several things. First, it could mean that we have to get serious. We have to concentrate. We have to simplify.

No pretense. No masks. No dressing up or trying to be someone we're not, but in complete honesty saying, "This one thing matters most. I need a fresh touch from God, and I am willing to give up some things if that's what it takes."

I think that's part of what it means to take off our ornaments.

But more importantly, in this text taking off ornaments also means something else. In ancient civilizations people put *on* their ornaments for idol worship. The Israelites put *on* their ornaments to worship the golden calf. And so by taking off their ornaments, they were admitting that they had been worshipping idols.

If we want to experience a personal revival, the first thing we've got to do is to ruthlessly examine our lives for idols.

What is an idol?

The simplest definition of an idol I've ever heard came from a pastor in Manhattan (New York City) named Tim Keller. He said, "An idol is anything you require in addition to God to be happy."

It doesn't get any clearer than that. An idol is not just a little stone statue that you keep in your room or a Buddha tummy that you rub for good luck. An idol is anything you require in your life in addition to God for you to be happy.

It's whenever we say, "I've got God in my life, but I have to have *that*, too, or I won't be satisfied." *That* person, *that* job, *that* acceptance, *that* toy—*that* whatever is an idol.

One of the things I noticed about this chapter is that God keeps referring to the Israelites as "stiff-necked people." "Stiff-necked" is not a phrase we use every day. We might not call it stiff-necked today. We might call it hardheaded.

You can almost hear God say, "You are a hardheaded people. You want what you want, when you want it. And if you don't get it, you're unhappy."

If you think about it, to be stiff-necked and hardheaded is the same thing as having an idol.

Why?

Because demanding to have God + *that* (whatever *that* is) means our hearts aren't tender. It means our wills aren't pliable. It means we are stiff-necked and hardheaded.

And that's what makes us demanding. That's what makes us grumpy. That's what makes us worried. That's why a lot of people are not experiencing the power and presence of God the way they really want to.

After carefully studying the Hebrew Scriptures, I have come to the conclusion that every time the glory of God left Israel, it always had something to do with idols.

Don't skip over that last sentence too quickly.

If you want the glory of God in your life, you have to ruthlessly examine your heart and ask, "What are the main reasons I get upset, edgy, indifferent, impatient, or anxious? What is in my life about which I repeatedly say, 'Anything but *that*, Lord!'?"

Search your heart. Take an inventory. God will help you identify the things that you insist on in addition to him as a requirement for your happiness.

Then with a great deal of prayer and serious reflection, ask the Lord, "How am I being stiff-necked and hardheaded? How can I smash that idol?"

If you don't destroy your idols, your idols will destroy you.

● ● ●

The second thing the Israelites did in response to God's statement to Moses was to make a new tent of meeting.

> Now Moses used to take a tent and pitch it outside the camp some distance away, calling it the "tent of meeting." Anyone inquiring of the LORD would go to the tent of meeting outside the camp. (Exod. 33:7)

I don't want to put words in God's mouth, but the intimation of this text is that God had finally reached the point where he said, "I'm not going to dwell in the main camp anymore. These people are so stiff-necked and hardheaded that my holiness might consume them."

So Moses put up a tent of meeting outside the camp.

What is so interesting about this tent of meeting is that the Israelites already had a place designated to worship God. It was called the tabernacle, and it was to be in the center of the camp.[4] Sometimes "tent of meeting" and "tabernacle" are used interchangeably in the Hebrew language. But what seems clear in this instance is that they are not the same.

The tabernacle was constructed with very specific instructions and details. It was dedicated as a place to house the ark of the covenant. The tent of meeting, in this instance, was just a tent that Moses erected outside the camp. God would come and meet with Moses there and, on occasion, with other people as well.

Even though the tabernacle was yet to be completed, many scholars believe that since there was now some doubt about whether God was going to continue to remain in the Israelite community (see v. 3), Moses thought another venue to meet with God might be necessary.

So guess what Moses did? He set up a surrogate tent outside the camp where he, and whoever else wanted to, could meet with God.

If God was not coming into the main camp, then Moses was going to where God was. It was almost as if Moses made a decision that said, "Lord, if you're not coming to where we are, then I'm going to where you are."

Sometimes people say to me, "I'm so spiritually dry right now that I don't even pray. Why should I? I get so little out of it." I always want to respond, "You get so little out of it? Boy, does that sound like our world. I don't feel like it, so I'm not going to do it?"

I think the exact opposite. If God just gives me a little, I take it! If God just gives me a taste, I want it! If God says, "I will meet you over there," I go! And I stay there as long as possible.

I love that Joshua, Moses' young right-hand man, wouldn't even leave the tent (see v. 11). Moses went back and forth from the camp to the tent, but Joshua wouldn't leave! He experienced God's presence there in powerful ways, and he wanted to linger.

John Newton, an Anglican pastor and songwriter, once wrote a letter to a friend who was struggling to pray. He wrote, "If you think you get nothing by going to the throne of grace, you certainly aren't going to gain anything by not going to the throne of grace."[5]

I don't think this means that God plays hard to get. But I am coming to believe that if we are really going to see the glory of

God, if we really want to experience revival, some folks have to get hungry enough to seek it.

Moses was hungry for God.

Notice that even after God tells Moses, "My Presence will go with you" (v. 14), that is still not enough? Moses wants more. He says, "Now show me your glory" (v. 18).

What a request! Moses' spiritual fire is all right. His fire is burning. But he's unsatisfied with where he is. He wants more of God.

Did you know that the first sign of spiritual slippage in your life is being satisfied with where you are right now? When you've lost your passion for more of God, it is a sure sign that you need to tend your fire.

I think God is looking for people who want more than an experience; he is looking for people who really want *him*. These are people who want more than goose bumps on their arms; they want the glory of God to pass by.

● ● ●

I surrendered my life completely to Christ when I was nineteen years old. I was so spiritually hungry for God; it was as though I couldn't get enough.

I would often wake up in the middle of the night hungering for time with God. I would pray myself back to sleep. I was seeing miracle after miracle happen in my life and in the lives of people I was praying for. It was just an amazing season of growth for me.

Those first few months I would come home from work around five in the evening. Christi, my wife, was working at a local bank and so she often didn't come home until after seven.

We lived in a little house in Bethany, Oklahoma, on Thirty-sixth and Rockwell. I couldn't wait to come home so I could read my Bible and pray. I would lie on my bed and read God's Word like a starving man trying to find bread. Every verse was like God shouting with a megaphone in my ear.

I remember one night I was reading from 1 Peter. I suddenly couldn't stop crying. I was so filled with assurance that I was forgiven, that I was God's son, and that he was pleased with me. God was showing me his glory, and I wanted more.

One morning I was sitting at our little dinette table in the kitchen. It was still dark outside. I was reading my devotions out of a devotional book called *Come Ye Apart*. I read from Isaiah: "For I will pour water on the thirsty land, and streams on the dry ground" (44:3).

And the floodgates opened again. I was completely filled up with the love of God, but I wanted more. I wanted God to show me his glory. My life was saturated with the good and beautiful God, but it wasn't enough. I wanted more water.

That was almost thirty years ago. A lot has changed since then. God has matured my faith. But that's still the kind of passion I want to have in my life.

I'll be honest with you. Sometimes I am most convicted that perhaps my greatest sin is my faint desire for the glory of God.

I want you to think about that. Do you need to repent of your lack of desire for God?

I think God is looking for some people who will go to the tent and say, "Even if I get very little out of this, I'm staying until God comes down. And I'm going to take whatever God gives me. God deserves my time and my attention. I am going to seek him! And if it takes thirty days, thirty weeks, thirty months, or thirty years, I'm going to be here. Let your face shine on me, Lord!"

If we want revival in our lives, we have to mourn a little bit. We have to take off our ornaments and go strong after our idols. We have to grieve for our lack of desire and seek God until the desire returns.

And when we do, you just never know—the glory of God might pass by.

7

GETTING PAST YOUR PAST

JOSHUA 2:1-24; 6:22-25

Life can only be understood backwards;
but it must be lived forwards.
–Søren Kierkegaard[1]

ACCORDING to rabbinical tradition, she was one of the four most beautiful women in the ancient world.

Not only was she recognized for her surpassing beauty, but also she was known for her incredible faith. Of all the great women in Israel's history, she is mentioned more often in the New Testament than any other woman except for Sarah, the wife of Abraham (see Matt. 1:5; Heb. 11:31; James 2:25). She became a greatly revered woman of God, so revered, in fact, that her face is on the Mount Rushmore of Old Testament faith heroes.

But she didn't start out that way, because she was a woman with a past.

Everyone, of course, has a past. Everyone lives with a tainted history of some kind. All of us have things we wish we had not done.

But there are some people who live with a *painful* past. A past they hope is buried so deep that no one will ever discover it. Or a past that people are keenly aware of, and no matter how much they try to put it behind them, there are certain folks who just won't let them forget.

Maybe you know the kind of past I'm referring to. The past that weighs so heavy, it feels as though it's crushing you. The past that is so shameful, it feels as though it's suffocating you.

People with that kind of past wonder, *Will I ever be free of the guilt and shame I feel? Will I ever* feel *forgiven? Can I ever get "past" my past?*

Christians know that Jesus came to forgive and redeem our past and to give us a glorious future. God's grace sets us free from the bondage of our past mistakes and gives us a new beginning.

If God can do that for a woman named Rahab, God can do that for you.

● ● ●

The setting of Rahab's story happened thirty-five hundred years ago. Forty years before that, God had delivered his people from the bondage of Egyptian slavery. However, since that deliverance, by their own decisions, the people of God have been wandering around as nomads in the desert.

But this is a new moment. They are on the brink of the Promised Land.

And so Joshua called his leaders around him and said, "Go through the camp and tell the people, 'Get your provisions ready. Three days from now you will cross the Jordan here to go in and take possession of the land the LORD your God is giving you for your own'" (Josh. 1:11).

There was only one thing standing in their way. A city called Jericho.

Jericho is considered one of the oldest cities in the world. There is evidence of some kind of a settlement there dating back to nine thousand BC. It was a massive city for its time, with thousands of people living in and around it. Consequently, it was the most well-protected and fortified city in Canaan.

It was built on a large mound of earth surrounded by an embankment with a stone retaining wall twelve to fifteen feet high at its base. On top of this retaining wall was another wall that was about twenty-five feet tall. Then at the top of that wall was another wall, forty-five feet higher than that.

That meant if you were standing at the bottom looking up, you would see a wall that was over seventy feet tall and so thick it was said you could ride two chariots side by side at the top. It was truly a daunting sight.

Joshua recognized the gargantuan challenge of Jericho. He sent two spies to do some recon for their army—clearly, a very dangerous job. "'Go, look over the land,' he said [to them], 'especially Jericho.' So they went and entered the house of a prostitute named Rahab and stayed there" (2:1).

• • •

This is the first time Rahab's name is mentioned in the Bible. And immediately we know of three strikes against her.

Strike One—Rahab Was a Woman

Why would that be a strike against her? In ancient times, women were looked down on. They had very little dignity and certainly no authority.

There was actually a prayer called the Berakah (ber-aw-kaw), or Blessing, that went like this: "Blessed are you, O Lord, King of the Universe, for not having made me a *Gentile*. Blessed are you, O Lord, King of the Universe, for not having made me a *slave*. Blessed are you, O Lord, King of the Universe, for not having made me a *woman*."[2] And this prayer was prayed by Jewish men every day.

Rahab was not a man; she was a woman.

Strike Two—Rahab Was a Canaanite

The Canaanites[3] were the people who lived in that land (also known as Gentiles). They were notorious for being very crude, cruel, and pagan. They were also very polytheistic and worshipped a pantheon of gods. Historians have identified at least twenty-four different gods worshipped by the Canaanites. That's a lot of gods to try and keep happy.

Rahab was not a Jew; she was a Canaanite.

Strike Three—Rahab Was a Prostitute

Being a prostitute meant that in the grand scheme of things, she was not even a very good woman or a good Canaanite.

She was a prostitute; she sold her body for money.

There were two kinds of prostitutes in that period. There was the temple prostitute, also known as a *qedeshah*.[4] *Qedeshah*s were used in religious rituals of worship to the Canaanite gods. They were slightly more acceptable in their society than the other kind of prostitute.

The second kind of prostitute was the basic streetwalker, hooker-type prostitute known as a *zonah*. Being on the lowest rung of prostitutes, *zonah*s were on the streets every night trading sexual favors for payment.

Guess which kind Rahab was?

She was a *zonah*. She was the lower-rung kind of prostitute. She was a lady of the night, who apparently was running a shady business that was well known in town.

It's interesting that many of the early commentators on Joshua tried to de-emphasize that fact by saying things such as,

Rahab wasn't really a prostitute; she was more like an innkeeper.

Rahab wasn't really a prostitute; she was just a person who owned a hotel where prostitution sometimes happened.

One ancient commentator named Rashi actually said she was really someone who just sold food to establishments like brothels so the prostitutes could eat.[5]

How compassionate of her.

No! Rahab was a prostitute!

She was a common harlot who sold her body on the street to make a living. And the Bible never tries to tell us she was anything but that.

Rahab is mentioned eight times in Scripture. Five of those eight times she is identified by what she did for a living. Five of those eight times she is called "Rahab the prostitute" or "Rahab the harlot." The Bible doesn't try to make her more noble, dignified, or righteous than she was.

She had a reputation. She was known for what she did for a living. She had a past.

● ● ●

Now how these two Israelite spies ended up on her doorstep is another matter. We can only speculate.

Maybe they thought her business actually was a hotel at the end of town. Maybe they thought it was a place where a lot of men could come and go and not be recognized. If they showed up in other places in town, they would have been instantly recognized by their accent or their appearance. So where better could they blend in than a place with a lot of other men who didn't want to be seen?

Or maybe they ended up there because it was the providence of God for the sake of Israel and for the sake of Rahab. All we know is that they showed up at her door, and Rahab instantly recognized that they were not from around there.

It would not have been uncommon for men from different cities to frequent a house of prostitution. But the city of Jericho was already on high alert that the Israelites were coming, and so everybody in the city was on the lookout for them.

The king of Jericho even got word that some strange men who looked a lot like Israelites had been seen at Rahab's place. So the king sent over some of the Jericho CIA to check it out.

They said to Rahab, "We know some Israelite soldiers have come to spy on our city. Why don't you go ahead and turn them over to us?" (see Josh. 2:3).

But for whatever reason, Rahab was anticipating this and had already made a decision. The Bible says she convinced the two Israelite spies that danger was imminent and had already taken them up onto the roof and hidden them under bundles of flax.

Bundles of flax? More on that in a moment.

Then at great risk to herself, Rahab concocted a story to the Jericho CIA that the men *had* been there but had already left the city and that if the agents hurried, they might be able to catch them.

Remarkably, the CIA agents believed her, because they didn't search the house and they rushed out of the city in hot pursuit of two phantoms trying to escape.

That was a very dangerous thing for Rahab to do, because if it were ever discovered that she aided and abetted the enemy by hiding them, protecting them, or covering for them, she would be considered a traitor, and that would bring certain death to her and her family.

Why would she take that kind of risk?

For the first time in her life, Rahab was being drawn to something more real than all the idols in Jericho. For years she had lived with a label—a label of degradation and disgrace. She had given away so much of herself that she didn't know if she had any of her *true* self left.

But now she was being drawn by a grace that was capturing her heart. Faith was being born in a woman who had given up on hope. And we know that because of what happened next.

• • •

When the CIA left Rahab's house, she went back up to the roof and had an amazing conversation with the Israelite spies.

> She . . . said to them, "I know that the LORD has given you this land and that a great fear of you has fallen on us, so that all who live in this country are melting in fear because of you." (Josh. 2:8-9)

Rahab is the first Gentile to profess faith in the name of the Lord God Almighty. She said, "I know. I know that the Lord has already done for you what he said he was going to do."

> We have heard how the LORD dried up the water of the Red Sea for you when you came out of Egypt. (V. 10)

She is recalling a miracle that happened before she was even born.

> [And we heard] what you did to Sihon and Og, the two kings of the Amorites east of the Jordan, whom you completely destroyed. (V. 10)

These were two powerful armies that came against Israel to try and stand in Israel's way, but by the power of God they were defeated.

And then Rahab the prostitute becomes Rahab the believer.

> The LORD your God is God in heaven *above* and on the earth *below*. (V. 11, emphasis added)

The greatest declaration of faith in the entire book of Joshua comes from Rahab of all people! She acknowledges her faith in the one true God; she declares he is supreme over all; and despite the odds stacked against her, she has faith to believe that this God can deliver on his promises.

And so she says to the spies, "I'll make a deal with you. I know the Lord is delivering this city to you. I know this city will be defeated by the army of the Lord. But I want your God to be my God. And I am going to act on my faith by showing loving-kindness to you in advance, so that you might show loving-kindness to me and my house" (see vv. 12-13).

And the spies reply, "Sounds good to us." And they make a covenant with her (see v. 14).

Rahab helps them escape by letting them rappel down the city wall with a rope through her window. But before they leave, something very interesting happens.

The spies tell her, "When we attack this city, it's going to get messy. It's going to be chaotic, and we have to have a way to protect you. So here's what we want you to do. Take this scarlet fabric, this crimson cord that you use to identify your profession, and tie it in your window. And when we see the red cord hanging over your house, we will *pass over it*. We will spare your life, and destruction will not come to you or anybody who is with you" (see vv. 17-20).

The scarlet cord was what prostitutes hung on their doors and windows to let people know they were ready for business. It was the beginning of the red-light district.

But don't miss this.

There is also a very intentional allusion to another story in Israel's salvation history, about the time when God was about to rescue Israel from Egypt. On the final night before their exodus, God's angel was going to pass through the land and strike down every firstborn Egyptian. However, God said if the Israelites would take the blood of a lamb and wipe it on the doorposts of their homes, death would *pass over* their house, and they would be saved.

We also know that Passover is being alluded to here because flax (remember the flax?), the plant Rahab used to cover the spies on her roof, was used at harvesttime to bring a wave offering to the Lord on the first Sunday of Passover.

This has *huge* implications for what God was doing in that moment for Rahab. God was providing for her protection and her deliverance by covering her house with a red cord of mercy.

Here's where it gets good.

God takes what has been the symbol of her *sin* (the first red-light district) and exchanges it for a symbol of her *salvation*.

I hope you won't *pass over* that last sentence too quickly.

She believed God's words, she put her trust in his salvation, and she acted on it with her faith. H. Orton Wiley, one of the great Wesleyan-Holiness theologians, said, "There is no clearer evidence of salvation by faith than this event."[6]

● ● ●

The end of the story is nothing short of miraculous.

> Now the gates of Jericho were securely barred because of the Israelites. No one went out and no one came in.

Then the LORD said to Joshua, "See, I have delivered Jericho into your hands, along with its king and its fighting men." (Josh. 6:1-2)

Then God commanded Israel's army to march around the entire city without speaking. The only sound they were to make was that issuing from the trumpets of the priests advancing before the ark of the covenant of the Lord.

It seemed like an odd way to win a battle, but the people obeyed. They marched in silence around the entire city, and they returned to their camp. The next day they did the very same thing.

They did this for six straight days.

On the seventh day, they went through the same ritual, only this time they marched around the city seven times. The seventh time around, when the priests sounded the trumpet blast, all the people shouted with one voice and the walls of mighty Jericho fell flat to the ground! And every Israelite charged into the city.

Now picture this.

The fight is raging, and people are screaming, shouting, and running. But in the middle of the mayhem, Joshua turns to the two Israelite spies and says, "Don't forget about Rahab. Somebody go get Rahab!"

But Joshua spared Rahab the prostitute, along with her family and everyone who was with her. Her family has lived in Israel *ever since.* (V. 25, ISV, emphasis added)

I love those words "ever since." They pack so much meaning.

Rahab has been saved from death, but does she have a life now to be saved for?

She has a past. She has been used and abused. Would anybody ever want her again? Would she have any chance for a family? Or was she relegated to what has been?

• • •

Joshua and the Israelite army go on to defeat city after city as God leads them. Rahab and her family are just tagging along with the Israelites, existing in a pathetic little pup tent but living very separate lives because nobody knows how to integrate them into the family. Jews and Canaanites don't coexist.

But then one day an Israelite guy named Salmon sees Rahab and thinks, *You know, she's kinda cute.* And he gets up his nerve to ask her out: "Do you want to grab a cup of coffee sometime? What about tomorrow?"

Before long, this Jewish guy is falling in love with used-up Rahab who has a past. And this can't be right, because Jews weren't supposed to marry anybody from outside the nation—especially somebody with a shady past like hers!

Well, Salmon eventually marries Rahab. And get the picture—there's thousands of Jews travelling around, lots of couples for God to choose from. But God says, "I'm choosing Salmon and Rahab."

And they have a son named Boaz, who marries a woman named Ruth.

And Boaz and Ruth have a son named Obed, who has a son named Jesse, who has a son named David, who becomes the king of Israel.

And twenty-eight generations later, a young couple from this same family tree, named Joseph and Mary, have a son named Jesus of Nazareth.

And somehow, by the grace of God, Rahab, "the Unwanted"; Rahab, "the Messed-Up"; Rahab, "the Used-Up"; Rahab, "the Shady Lady with a Past" . . . became the great-great-grandmother of the Messiah![7]

And her family has lived in Israel "ever since."

We serve an "ever since" God, who doesn't just want to save us from death; our God wants to save us for life!

Rahab had a past that she had created for herself. God had a future he was creating for her.

I love that about God. A lot of people today wouldn't invite Rahab over to their house for dinner. But God says, "I am making her part of *my* story."

And you know what? She was the perfect choice, because we are all people with a past. We deserve condemnation for what we've done. But God rescues us out of our past and gives us what we did not deserve—a future with him.

That future is created because God's own Son died on the cross for our sins, and blood covered his head, his hands, and his feet. The Paschal Lamb on Golgotha's hill was the Lamb of God who became "the atoning sacrifice for our sins, and not only for ours but also for the sins of the whole world" (1 John 2:2).

● ● ●

Let me ask you, "What's your label?"[8]

Joe, "the Liar"?

Susan, "the Arrogant"?

Steve, "the Addicted"?

Melissa, "the Insecure"?

Whatever is attached to your name, I want to tell you something very important: you don't need to get your act together; you need a Savior!

The story of Rahab is extremely important for us to understand because this is what it tells us: God saves sinners *while* they are still sinners! *Not* after they get their acts together. *Not* after they straighten up. But *when* they put their faith in Jesus.

God is in the business of taking the symbols of our sin and exchanging them for the symbols of our salvation.

Martin Luther called it the "great exchange." He urged us to pray, "Lord Jesus, you are my righteousness, just as I am your sin. You have taken upon yourself what is mine and have given me what is yours. You have taken upon yourself what you were not and have given me what I was not."

Your past might be a problem for you, but it's not a problem for God. You do have a past, but God holds your new future.

Rahab made the family tree of Jesus. So can you.

MINI-ME

JUDGES 6-7

We can easily forgive a child who is afraid of the dark; the
real tragedy of life is when men are afraid of the light.
–Plato[1]

WHEN SOMEONE feels worthless as a person, it has something
to do with how he or she views God.

If you have a *small* view of God, chances are you have a small view
of yourself. If you have a *big* view of God, chances are you have
a healthy view of yourself. The "smallness" or "bigness" of your
God determines how you think about who *you* are.

Mini-Me is a character in a movie. He is a short little man who is
the smaller version of Dr. Evil. He's exactly the same as Dr. Evil
in every way, except he is one-eighth the size. He is Mini-Me.

There are a lot of Christians who have the Mini-Me mentality. They are greatly reduced versions of the real selves God has
made them to be. They feel insignificant and insecure about what

they are capable of accomplishing even with God's help. And they have limited God's power in their lives to the narrow confines of what they personally feel they are capable of doing.

Here is the big idea: the way we live is a direct result of the size of our God.

This means the primary problem for most of us is that we are not fully convinced we are absolutely safe in the hands of a completely competent, all-knowing, ever-present, utterly loving, infinitely *big* God.

If you wake up every morning and go through the day with a Mini-Me view of yourself, then you'll have a Mini-Me view of God. And there are going to be consequences.

You will live in fear and anxiety because you aren't convinced of God's power.

You will be defensive and overly sensitive to others' opinions of you because you aren't convinced of your identity in Christ.

You will find it difficult to pray because you will begin to wonder if prayer really changes things and can make a difference.

Pastor John Ortberg said, "When human beings shrink God, they offer prayer without faith, worship without awe, serve without joy, suffer without hope, and the result is a life of stagnation and fear, a loss of vision, an inability to persevere and see it through."[2]

Thankfully, we do not serve a Mini-Me God. Whatever your need, God is bigger. Whatever your weakness, God is stronger. The story of Gideon teaches us how to break free from the Mini-Me syndrome.

● ● ●

An angel of the Lord paid a visit to a man named Gideon while he was threshing wheat in a winepress. This begs the question, "Why was he threshing wheat in a winepress?" You might be thinking, *I thought winepresses were places where people made wine.* And you would be right.

An ancient winepress was mainly just a rock pit. The winemakers would throw a bunch of grapes into the bottom of the pit. Then they would dance around on top of the grapes with their bare feet until they had trampled them flat and all the juice was squeezed out. Stomping on the grapes with your bare feet was also a good way to begin the fermenting process, because whatever was in between your toes would mix in with the juice.[3]

At the bottom of the winepress was a little gulley where the juice would flow over into a container of some sort, and you would have the beginning of wine.

That's how winepresses worked.

A threshing floor was a place where people sifted wheat. It was usually a large area with a stone base. You wanted it to be where the wind could really blow. You've heard of separating the wheat from the chaff? That meant that when you threw the wheat up in the air, the wind would blow the chaff away, and because the grain was heavier than the chaff, it would fall back to the ground.

So there are winepresses, and there are threshing floors.

Usually people wouldn't think about threshing wheat in a winepress. Actually, a winepress would be a lousy place to thresh wheat. On the one hand, it would be way too small, and on the other hand, if you were down in a pit, the wind couldn't carry off the chaff.

Point made.

So what is Gideon doing threshing wheat in a winepress?

He's hiding. He's hiding because he's afraid of the Midianites.

The Midianites were Israel's enemies from the east. They were strong, powerful, and many. Hordes of them would swoop into the Promised Land by the *thousands* right around harvesttime to steal the crops that the Israelites had worked so hard to raise.

The text says they came rushing in like "swarms of locusts" and "invaded the land to ravage it" (Judg. 6:5). And they did this for seven years straight, leaving Israel in a desperate situation. The Israelites were so frightened they would actually take refuge in caves and holes in the ground.

That's why Gideon is hiding. He is terrified that the Midianites are going to find out where he is and steal his pitiful little stash of wheat away from him.

Do you see how pathetic this scene is?

Gideon is not G.I. Joe with the Kung-Fu Grip. He's not Brave-heart. He's not even Samson. He is Mini-Me Man, who has zero confidence in himself and very little confidence in God.

The angel of the Lord came to him and said, "The LORD is with you, mighty warrior" (v. 12).

Mighty warrior? Good one, Lord. Big coward? Yes. Gutless wonder? Probably. But mighty warrior? That might be stretching it just a bit.

Gideon knows he's not a mighty warrior. And *God* knows he's not a mighty warrior. But here we learn an important truth about our faith: *we* see ourselves for who we are; *God* sees us for what we can become. God always sees more in us than we see in ourselves.

God: "By yourself, Gideon, you are a scared, frightened little man. But with *me*, you are a mighty warrior."

Gideon: "But, Lord, can't you see who I am? Can't you see the situation I'm in? Can't you see how small I am?"

God: "I know what's going on here. But I want you to go with the strength you've got and save Israel from Midian."

Then God said five important words.

God: "Am *I* not sending you?" (v. 14, emphasis added).

Gideon: "But, Lord . . ."

This is the third time in the narrative that Gideon has used the word "but." Which shouldn't surprise us, because "but" is the most common word in the Mini-Me vocabulary.

"But, Lord . . ."

"But, how . . .?"

"But, why . . .?"

> Gideon replied, "[But, Lord,] how can I save Israel? My clan is the weakest in Manasseh, and I am the least in my family." (V. 15)

Gideon had been conditioned to see himself in a certain way. He had been programmed to see himself as powerless enough to justify saying no to God's call on his life.

Gideon: "God, I can't be who you say I can be. I am the weakest person in the weakest family in the weakest tribe of Israel. I have no strength. I have no worth. I have no abilities. I'm a nobody!"

It's a litany of excuses that ignores the strength God is offering him and is really nothing more than a poorly disguised form of a self-centered existence.

But God is patient with Gideon. He doesn't say, "No, Gideon. You are a fine young man with all the talent in the world. You can do this!" Instead, God counters with a "but" of his own: "[But] I will be with you, and you will strike down all the Midianites" (v. 16).

This promise from God is the crucial hinge on which everything turns—not just for Gideon but also for you and me.

When we do what we *can*, God will do what we *can't*![4]

God: "Go with the strength you have, and I will be with you!"

If we will do what we *can*, God will do what we *can't*![5]

What is unthinkable and undoable on your own becomes unstoppable when it's God and you together. Because who is standing with you is far more important than what you're capable of alone.

• • •

I was not the "mighty warrior" type in the fifth grade. I had a soup-bowl haircut, wore little round glasses, and had arms so skinny that if I put on boxing gloves, they looked like giant Q-tips (imagine a scrawnier version of Harry Potter). I had Gideon written all over me.

Around this time our family had just moved to a new town, which meant a new school for me. I was doing my best to fit in but was not having much success. A few days after I arrived at the new school, I vividly remember that one of the class bullies tried to intimidate me.

I still remember the bully's name, Calvin—Calvin, "the Bully."

Calvin said to me on that first day, "I don't like new kids. You're going to wish we had never met."

To which I said, "I already do."

It was an honest answer. But Calvin said it was the wrong answer. He told me to meet him behind the gym after school. I told him I wasn't very good with directions. My sarcasm was an attempt to stay cool, but Calvin had accomplished his mission. I was sufficiently intimidated.

I started taking different routes home from school in hopes of not running into him. I avoided Calvin in the halls as much as possible. And for the next few weeks, I had a severe case of the Mini-Me mentality.

That is until I got to know my new neighbors.

Our neighbors were called the Camachos. Mr. and Mrs. Camacho had six children: Manuel, Philip, Angie, Helen, George, and Ricky. And Manuel, as it turned out, was the toughest kid in town. He was nineteen and still in high school. He had bulging biceps and wore tight T-shirts and a black stocking cap (without the little furry ball on top) year round. Nobody messed with Manuel, and I discovered nobody messed with his friends either.

For whatever reason, Manuel took me under his wing. Maybe he felt sorry for me. Maybe it was his contribution to society. It couldn't have been because I was that cool. He let me hang out with him. He played Nerf football with me in the street. We watched college football games together on Saturday afternoons. I became like a little nerdy brother to him.

I never told Manuel about Calvin. I didn't have to. I just felt like a different person. I knew that I had a strong friend nobody wanted to mess with and that he had my back.

And I learned that when it comes to self-confidence, it really matters who is standing with you.

Apparently, Calvin knew it too. When Calvin found out that Manuel and I liked to "hang" together, he never picked on me again.

● ● ●

I think that's what God was trying to say to Gideon: "I know what you've been, Gideon. I know you feel weak. And I know about the Midianites. But you don't have to hide anymore. You don't have to thresh your wheat in a winepress. You don't have to be afraid. I am with you! I am a great big God who will never ask you to do what I won't give you the power to accomplish."

With a promise like that, you can face any problem. It doesn't answer all of your questions about the nitty-gritty details. Notice there is nothing about when, how, where, or why—only about *who*.

God said, "*I* will be with you" (Judg. 6:16, emphasis added).

That is enough.

● ● ●

With that assurance, Gideon was ready for the big test. He did some recruiting and gathered up a group of men to go to war with the Midianites—32,000 in all.

That sounds like a pretty good-sized army, until you consider that the Midianites had an army of 135,000, not including camels (see

Judg. 8:10). That means Gideon was outnumbered by more than four to one.

God came to Gideon and said, "You've got serious number problems here."

Gideon probably said something such as, "God, I'm so glad to hear you say that, because I was afraid you were going to make me go into battle outnumbered four to one!"

And God said, "No, Gideon, I would never do that. You have way too many guys."

Or as the text puts it, "You have too many men. I cannot deliver Midian into their hands, or Israel would boast against me, 'My own strength has saved me'" (7:2).

I love that! "This is *my* battle, Gideon! And I don't want anyone in Israel taking credit for this victory by thinking they defeated the Midianites because it was only four-to-one odds. So here's what I want you to do. I want you to send home every soldier who's afraid."

You can only imagine Gideon's response to that mandate: "Lord, *everyone* is afraid. I won't have anybody left!"

Well, he was wrong. Only 22,000 of the troops went home, leaving Gideon with 10,000 soldiers. This made the odds even more outlandish than before—more than *thirteen* to one.

But God said, "That's still a bit high. We're going to have to reduce that number a little more."

Now you have to read this next part for yourself or you may think I'm making this up.

But the LORD said to Gideon, "There are still too many men. Take them down to the water, and I will thin them out for you there. If I say, 'This one shall go with you,' he shall go; but if I say, 'This one shall not go with you,' he shall not go."

So Gideon took the men down to the water. There the LORD told him, "Separate those who lap the water with their tongues as a dog laps from those who kneel down to drink." Three hundred of them drank from cupped hands, lapping like dogs. All the rest got down on their knees to drink.

The LORD said to Gideon, "With the three hundred men that lapped I will save you and give the Midianites into your hands. Let all the others go home." (Vv. 4-7)

So here's what Gideon is left with—going into battle against the powerful Midianite army with the dog-lappers.

It's funny to me how some Bible commentators try to make the case that the three hundred dog-lappers were deserving of this honor.

One commentator, who shall remain nameless, writes,

God saw how untrustworthy would be those thousands who carelessly indulged under the lure of the flesh, over against the three hundred who exemplified a spirit of vigilance and disciplined life in the Spirit. Thus were selected the strong and resolute, the men who could be trusted under rigorous conditions, those who did not think of themselves before the enemy's unexpected assault. This is ever the divine principle of selection for service. As Gideon, so the church in this day is served well by the minority group ready and vigilant.[6]

That sounds so good. So holy. So heroic. The problem with that whole line of thinking is that in the Bible, anytime someone is compared to a dog, or referred to as a dog, it's never a compliment. It's always a slam!

We like our dogs in America. We buy them little soft beds and squeaky toys. We give them baths and brush their fur. We praise them for going to the bathroom outside. We take family pictures with them at holidays. We like our dogs! But the Bible's culture is very different. Dogs were a public nuisance. Dogs were scavengers who roamed around at night dumping over garbage cans. It was not a compliment to be called a dog in Gideon's day.

So what did the dog-lappers represent?

One Old Testament scholar named Douglas Stuart puts it this way: "The idea most likely is that the guys who lap water like a dog drank in a way that we would think of as kind of geeky, kind of nerds."[7]

In other words, these were not the three hundred Spartans. These were not Israelite elite Special Forces. These are the three hundred dog-lappers. They were "300 geeky guys who would trip over their own swords."[8]

That's what God leaves Gideon with.

The whole point of God winnowing the troops down was to make clear that the victory was God's alone.

Midianite soldiers now outnumbered the Israelites 450 to 1. Read that again—450 to 1!

Meanwhile, Gideon and his three hundred dog-lapper soldiers surrounded the Midian army armed with torches and trumpets. And on a signal, they simultaneously blew their trumpets and lit their torches, which caused the Midianite camp to be thrown into such mayhem that they started killing each other. The Midianites took off running and never looked back.

Israel was free. And perhaps even more astonishing, Mini-Me Gideon had become a mighty warrior for God.

• • •

"This is my battle," God says. "So you don't have to live in fear."

You know, Gideon wasn't the only guy in the Bible who wrestled with fear. Pretty much all the faith giants did—Abraham, Moses, Joshua, David, Elijah, Jeremiah, Peter, all the disciples—everybody did.

In fact, the single most common command in the Bible is, "Fear not. Don't be afraid." Why? "Because I am with you."[9]

"Lord, can't you see how big the enemy is? Don't you see how dark the night is? Don't you know how weak I am?"

"But I am with you."

That's the secret to resisting the Mini-Me mentality. Circumstances can be swirling out of your control, but there's an inner reality that God is enough. He really is.

I think that is why Paul said, "I can do all this through him [Christ] who gives me strength" (Phil. 4:13). I can face anything life has to throw at me, including rejection, loneliness, beatings, and prison, through Christ "who gives me strength."

Nobody else and nothing else can give this sort of peace to you. Your circumstances can't give you this peace. Your natural abilities can't give you this peace. This peace comes from God.

This is God's good news for you in Christ:

"I am bigger than your problems."

"I am bigger than your failures."

"I am bigger than your regrets."

"I am bigger than your weaknesses."

God knows about the Midianites in your life.

He knows about your worries.

> He knows about your kids.

> He knows about the lost job.

He knows about the crumbling marriage.

> He knows about the affair.

> He knows about the abortion.

He knows about where you are stagnant.

> He knows where your dreams have died.

> He knows.

But he has better dreams for you. If you ask him, he will be a bigger presence in your life than you have ever known. And you don't have to be afraid anymore. God will make a way.

Who is standing with you really matters.

9

CHASING SARDINES

JUDGES 13-16

At times the whole world seems to be in conspiracy
to importune you with emphatic trifles.
–Ralph Waldo Emerson[1]

IT ALL STARTED so well for Samson. There were such high
hopes for him.

It began when an angel of the Lord came to his childless parents
and announced his birth. That puts him in very good scriptural
company: Isaac was announced to Abraham and Sarah, John the
Baptist was announced to Zechariah and Elizabeth, and Jesus was
announced to Mary and Joseph. Samson, too, was announced by
an angel.

The text also tells us that Samson's mother was barren, meaning
she not only had no children but was physically incapable of doing
so. So Samson's conception in itself was a miracle of God.[2]

And Samson was set apart as a Nazirite (not to be confused with
a Nazarene). The word "Nazirite" means one who is "separated,"

"consecrated," or "devoted." It signified someone who was specially dedicated for sacred service to God.

According to Numbers 6:1-8, a Nazirite was marked by three covenant vows to show his complete devotion to God: (1) he could not drink wine or any strong drink; (2) he could not touch anything that was dead, human or otherwise; and (3) he could not cut his hair—ever.

These were vows of purity, self-control, and separation.

A person who took a Nazirite vow could do so for a designated period or for a lifetime. Samuel was a lifelong Nazirite (see 1 Sam. 1–11). But as far as we know, Samson was the first Nazirite dedicated before he was born.

An angel announced his birth, he was conceived in a barren woman, and he was consecrated as a Nazirite from birth. It raises pretty high expectations for what Samson is going to accomplish in his life.

That's why it's so surprising that the first time we encounter him as an adult, he's already making questionable decisions.

● ● ●

The first surprise is who he wants to marry. "Samson went down[3] to Timnah and saw there a young Philistine woman. When he returned, he said to his father and mother, 'I have seen a Philistine woman in Timnah; now get her for me as my wife'" (Judg. 14:1-2).

The Philistines were bitter enemies of Israel from the southwest. The Philistines worshipped a god named Dagon. Goliath, the giant that David killed in battle, was a Philistine.

In essence, Samson wants to marry someone who doesn't share his faith in Yahweh God. And Samson's parents try to talk him out of it.

But we get a little clue into Samson's mind-set by what he says next: "Get her for me. She's the right one for me" (v. 3). That phrase literally means, "She is right in my eyes."

Interestingly, that is the exact phrase the writer of Judges uses over and over to refer to a problem Israel as a nation is facing: "Everyone did what was right in his own eyes" (21:25, NASB). It is a spiritual mentality that will cause Samson to break every vow he has made to God.

Notice what happens next.

> Samson went down[4] to Timnah together with his father and mother. As they approached the vineyards of Timnah, suddenly a young lion came roaring toward him. The Spirit of the LORD came powerfully upon him so that he tore the lion apart with his bare hands as he might have torn a young goat. But he told neither his father nor his mother what he had done. (14:5-6)

This is the first time we are made aware of what Samson is most known for. Samson is very strong. He is so strong that he can kill lions with his bare hands and hundreds of enemies in battle. Everybody is afraid of him. He has a reputation for being a mighty warrior. He is Conan the Barbarian without the Arnold Schwarzenegger accent.

But here's the irony of the story. Although Samson is physically very strong, morally he is deeply weak.

He is physically amazing but spiritually flawed. What makes him most dangerous is that he has great strength but no wisdom by which to use that strength. And Samson's lack of good sense, and absence of a moral and spiritual compass, will eventually lead to his downfall.

We see it coming by some interesting word pictures that begin to show up.

> Some time later, when he went back to marry her, he *turned aside* to look at the lion's carcass, and in it he saw a swarm of bees and some honey. He scooped out the honey with his hands and ate as he went along. When he rejoined his parents, he gave them some, and they too ate it. But he did not tell them that he had taken the honey from the lion's carcass. (Vv. 8–9, emphasis added)

Now at first glance, Samson stopping to get some honey seems harmless. He was hungry, and as guys are wont to do, he stopped on his road trip to get something sweet to snack on. That he wanted something sweet wasn't the point. It was *how* he got something to eat.

● ● ●

The first thing the narrator tells us is that Samson "turned aside" (Judg. 14:8).

"Turned aside" or "turned away" is often a biblical metaphor for someone who is off track—taken his or her eyes off of God—and who is on a path to destruction.

Do you remember when Moses came down from the mountain with the two tablets of the Ten Commandments in his hands?

The first thing he saw when he entered the camp of the Israelites was that they had built an idol to worship.

Notice what he says: "When I looked, I saw that you had sinned against the LORD your God; you had made for yourselves an idol cast in the shape of a calf. You had *turned aside* quickly from the way that the LORD had commanded you" (Deut. 9:16, emphasis added).

Later, when the prophet Samuel was about to die, he appointed his sons to succeed him as judges over Israel. But there was a problem. "His sons did not follow his ways. They *turned aside* after dishonest gain and accepted bribes and perverted justice" (1 Sam. 8:3, emphasis added).

Psalm 14 says, "The LORD looks down from heaven on all mankind to see if there are any who understand, any who seek God. All have *turned away*, all have become corrupt; there is no one who does good, not even one" (vv. 2–3, emphasis added).

Samson has "turned aside"; he has "turned away." He is off the path and is not where he's supposed to be. He has forgotten who he is, is distracted from his God-ordained purpose, and now is breaking his vows to God.

How does he do that?

● ● ●

The first vow he breaks is his vow not to drink wine or touch anything from the grapevine. We have a hint of trouble in Judges 14:5 when the text says Samson and his parents "approached the vineyards of Timnah." Samson is venturing down a path to temptation.

Then in verse 10 we're told that Samson has a bridegroom feast with thirty companions. A bridegroom's feast usually lasted for seven days and always included lots and lots of wine. In fact, they were literally called drinking festivals. Samson has a "feast" with thirty guy friends.

Nazirite vow number one is broken.

But it's not too late. Samson may have "turned aside" for a moment, but he can *turn back* to God. He doesn't have to continue down this path. But one decision leads to another.

The next thing Samson does is to take honey from a dead lion's carcass. Samson not only touches the dead animal but also completely internalizes it by eating it. And then he has the audacity to bring his parents in on the act by giving them the honey and not telling them where it came from.

Nazirite vow number two is broken.[5]

Do you see the cycle here? Samson has completely lost his way. He is doing "what is right in his own eyes" (see again Judg. 21:25, NASB).

Everything begins to spiral out of control. He ends up marrying the Philistine girl. He then makes a bet with his thirty Philistine drinking buddies at the bridegroom party that they can't solve his riddle. The bet is if they can solve his riddle, he will give them each a new set of clothes, but if they can't solve the riddle, they each have to give him a new set of clothes.

It's a bet—involving clothes. That's weird.

The guys can't figure the riddle out, and they get so angry about it that they secretly go to Samson's new wife and threaten to kill her and her family if she doesn't find out what the riddle means. She relentlessly tries to pry the answer out of Samson. She cries, whines, pouts, and begs. She tells him, "If you really loved me, you'd tell" (see 14:16). This marriage is not starting out on the right foot.

Finally, on the last day of the feast, he gives in and tells her. She immediately tells his thirty friends. They then come to Samson and tell him what the riddle means. And Samson answers them, "If you had not plowed with my heifer, you would not have solved my riddle" (v. 18).

Guys, just in case you were wondering, you're not going to win brownie points with your new bride by calling her a heifer on your honeymoon. Samson was actually using vulgar hip-hop language to belittle his wife and to tell his thirty friends where they could go.

And then, because Samson doesn't want to pay off the bet, he goes to the next city over, randomly kills thirty Philistines from a town called Ashkelon, strips off their clothes, and pays off his bet to the thirty drinking buddies. Then livid with anger, he leaves his new wife and goes back to his dad's house.

Some time passes. Samson cools off and decides to patch things up with his wife.

> Later on, at the time of wheat harvest, Samson took a young goat and went to visit his wife. (15:1)

That's Samson—the true romantic.[6]

> He said, "I'm going to my wife's room." But her father would not let him go in. "I was so sure you hated her," he said, "that I gave her to your companion [i.e., the best man at your

wedding]. Isn't her younger sister more attractive? Take her instead." (Vv. 1-2)

This is quickly moving into Jerry Springer territory.

Now look at what Samson says next: "This time I have a right to get even with the Philistines; I will really harm them" (v. 3).

Is Samson actually implying that perhaps his earlier killings had been reckless and wrong and that this time his murders would be justified? Is this rationalization at its most dangerous?

And so Samson does exactly what every normal guy does when he's upset and needs to vent.

> So he went out and caught three hundred foxes and tied them tail to tail in pairs. He then fastened a torch to every pair of tails, lit the torches and let the foxes loose in the standing grain of the Philistines. He burned up the shocks and standing grain, together with the vineyards and olive groves. (Vv. 4-5)

Samson has officially become a terrorist.

When the Philistines find out that Samson has burned their fields (in effect destroying their economy), they take revenge on him by taking his new wife and father-in-law and burning them to death. In retaliation to that, Samson goes and slaughters a bunch of Philistines. The Philistines decide Samson has gone too far this time, and they declare war against the entire nation of Israel.

Understandably, the people of Israel are upset. So they decide to send a delegation to Samson to ask why he is so out of control.

Samson responds to their query by saying, "I merely did to them what they did to me" (v. 11).

And now we see the depth of Samson's character. He cannot rise above the next act of retaliation. He cannot stop the insanity.

He is so self-deceived that he no longer sees how his own decisions have contributed to the terrible situation he is in. And he can't see that he has put his own people at terrible risk.

Do you know anybody like that? No matter how badly he or she behaves, it's always somebody else's fault. Somebody else is always to blame.

"She did this to me, and that's why I am the way I am."

How did Samson get to the place he finds himself now? How could a guy who had so much going for him, so much promise and potential, end up so out of control?

• • •

A few summers ago we had a very large spider living on our front porch. We called her Charlotte. She would hide during the day, but in the early evening she would come down right in front of our porch entrance and build magnificent webs—immense, intricate webs.

We chose to leave her alone, because, we thought, she was working hard, catching unwanted insects, and keeping unwanted people away at night.

One morning I got up very early to go for a run. It was still dark outside. I stepped out onto the front porch, did a little bit of stretching, and then launched out. But I completely forgot about Charlotte's web and ran face first into it.

Have you ever walked into a spider's web? If you have, you already know what I did. I freaked out! I'm glad it was early in the morning, because if any of my neighbors had seen me dancing around, they would have thought I had completely lost my mind.

Now, I knew that her web was there. I had seen it many times. I had even gotten used to it. But the darker it was, the less I could see, and it just went off my radar screen.

Darkness makes you run into a lot of bad things.

● ● ●

I think that's how "turning aside" works.

It should never surprise us when we run into life's spiderwebs. We can see them building every day. But when we continually choose to break our vows to God, we eventually get so used to them that we don't think about them anymore. And one day everything finally becomes so dark that we launch out and find ourselves right in the middle of them.

That's how people turn aside. That's the way it works.

It should never surprise us.

Here is the truth of this story: small compromises lead to big consequences.

Seemingly insignificant decisions matter. Every life choice is a decision either to turn *toward* God or to turn *aside* from God. And sometimes the path can be so gradual that you can go a very long way without realizing just how far you've wandered.

● ● ●

I heard about an unusual incident that happened on the West Coast some years ago when some whales were beached. They came in too close to shore, and when the tide went out, the whales were stuck on the sand.

What was so unusual was that there were three hundred whales beached at the same *time* and in the same *place*. Sadly, before anyone could get the whales back in the water, all three hundred had died. Nobody could figure out why this very strange thing had happened until some marine biologists discovered that the whales had accidentally grounded themselves on the beach because they were chasing sardines.

They all died.

Have you ever seen a sardine? Do you know how small a sardine is compared to a whale? People put sardines on their pizza! But even a tiny sardine can bring a whale to its death if the whale keeps chasing it long enough.

This is a living parable of the life of Samson. He has unlimited resources and expansive God-given abilities, but he wastes his life chasing little things that were "right in his own eyes."

He was a whale chasing sardines.

If we chase after anything smaller than God, it will eventually destroy us.

For God's sake—for your sake—stop chasing sardines.

BEAUTY AND THE BEAST

1 SAMUEL 25

You make beautiful things out of the dust. . . .
You make beautiful things out of us.
–Michael Gungor[1]

THIS STORY BEGINS with the introduction of two people. One is a beauty; the other is a beast. One is a villain; the other is a hero.

The beast was a man named Nabal.

The first thing we discover about Nabal is that he was incredibly wealthy. He dealt in both capital and commodities. He owned land and flocks. We're not told how he came to be so rich, but we know his prosperity was his primary identity. We know that by how he is introduced. Only after being told of his riches are we told his name. Nabal's possessions precede his very person. His life is determined by his property.

Not only do we know about Nabal's wealth and priorities, but we also know something about his personality. He is characterized as uncouth and ill behaved. He was mean and dishonest. He was rude and crude. His name says it all. In the Hebrew, *nabal* literally means "fool," and it fit his character well.

A *nabal* is a stupid, simpleminded clod, but not in a harmless way like Forrest Gump or Michael Scott from *The Office*. A *nabal* is a vicious, mean-spirited person who not only lacks manners and etiquette but is a spiritual, moral, and social disaster as well.

A *nabal* is not just cruel, like Joseph Stalin or Idi Amin, but mean and idiotic. Think Archie Bunker, Al Bundy, and Dwight Schrute all wrapped into one.

Nabal was the Bunker/Bundy/Schrute of landowners, who cared for no one but himself. He was a good-for-nothing loudmouth who couldn't have a reasonable conversation with anyone.

To be called a fool in the Bible is no small thing. Fool is the Bible's most contemptuous term. The fool is a person who is clueless to what God is doing in the world, not because he or she is ignorant and searching, or lost and looking for help. But because fools claim to know it all, have it all figured out, and think they know the ropes.

Psalm 14:1 says, "The fool says in his heart, 'There is no God.'" Fools are people who have come to think of themselves as independent and self-sufficient, and they believe they can do whatever they please. Isaiah 32 describes a *nabal* as a person who refuses to help people in need. All they care about are themselves, and they seem incapable of concern about anything outside of their orbit.

Jesus told a story about a rich fool in Luke 12:13-21. He was a man who had barns filled to overflowing, with more than enough for himself and plenty to go around. Without consulting God and with no regard for anyone else, he decided more was better and built a bigger barn. He lived his life as if there were no God and died as if there were no God, because he hadn't stopped long enough to notice there are no U-Hauls behind hearses.

That's the basic problem for fools. Everything a fool works for eventually caves in. In fact, the Hebrew verb from which "fool" is derived means "to collapse." When the hot air has left the gaudy red balloon, all that's left is a shriveled, deflated ego. That is the destiny of a fool. And so not only was his name Nabal but also he *was* a *nabal*.

But we're also told something else about him. He happened to stumble into an incredibly fortunate marriage arrangement, because Nabal, "the Beast," married way over his head.

Nabal's wife is the Beauty of the story. Her name was Abigail.

Abigail was the complete opposite of her husband. She was clever, intelligent, and beautiful. Not only was she outwardly striking, but she was inwardly attractive as well. She was perceptive, insightful, and wise. Abigail *acts* and *speaks* for God in this story, and her actions and words turn out to be God's salvation for the future king of Israel.

That's when David enters the story. David was on the move, hiding in caves and running for his life in the wilderness. Like Moses before him and Jesus after him, David had things to learn in the wilderness that could be learned in no other way.

One of the things he learned during his wilderness years was the value of community. He began to draw a ragged group of people around him. Their number soon swelled to six hundred men, plus their wives and children. These people weren't exactly the cream of the crop. First Samuel 22:2 tells us the sociological profile of David's little band: "in debt," "in distress," and "discontented." They were all misfits who couldn't make it in regular society.

Rejects.

Losers.

Dropouts.

Not exactly the kind of folks you want to build an empire around.

But under David's leadership, the six hundred men had been turned into a tight-knit band of guerilla fighters, roaming the wilderness of Paran to protect shepherds from the predatory raids of the desert's wild tribes. David and his merry men were serving as a kind of Robin Hood operation, because in addition to the natural dangers of wilderness living, it was also a high-crime district. Bandits and outlaws lived in the wilderness, preying on travelers, plundering the defenseless.

One of Jesus' most famous stories is about a traveler in the Judean wilderness getting robbed, beaten, and then rescued by a Samaritan. That's the kind of work David and his men were doing. They were the first Good Samaritans. Eugene Peterson says they were an unofficial neighborhood watch group.[2] And among the many they had helped were the herdsmen of Nabal.

Sheepshearing time rolled around. That was the equivalent of harvest for the farmers. It was a time to cash in on their investments. For most people, it was a season of generosity and goodwill—a time to share their blessings with others. It was a common custom, much like our practice of tipping restaurant servers, that when the sheep were sheared, the owner of the flock would pay a portion of his profit to those who had protected his shepherds.

So David sent ten of his men to talk with Nabal about his army's need for food and clothing. It seemed like a reasonable request in light of all that David had done for him. As David saw it, Nabal would have had far fewer sheep to shear if he and his men had not served as voluntary protectors of Nabal's flocks and herds.

Not only that, David and his men had probably existed on survival rations all year. The wilderness wasn't exactly a smorgasbord for food supplies. Some of Nabal's fresh fruit and baked pastries would have been a welcomed change. It was not only fair to pay the laborers their hire but also the right thing to do.

But when Nabal heard the request, he acted as if he had never even heard of David. He lumped him in with the riffraff of desert outlaws who were always going around with their hands out. He called David a no-account runaway slave leading a bunch of nobodies who weren't worth the ground they were standing on. And so Nabal said they had no right to *his* bread, *his* meat, and *his* water!

Nabal wasn't just stupid enough to deny David. He insulted him in the process and embarrassed him. He humiliated, disgraced, and made light of him. He "Dwight Schrute'd" him!

It would be like you reaching out to help someone in need, not because he or she had asked for help, but out of the goodness of your heart. And when that person got back on his or her feet, you asked him or her for a lesser favor. And not only did that person reject your request, but he or she also sneered in your face. It's one thing to be ungrateful. It's another thing to be mocked in the process.

When David heard Nabal's response, he completely lost it! He blew his stack! David's honor was at stake. As far as he was concerned, there was only one way to deal with an obnoxious, ungrateful hardhead. He told his men: "Get your swords! We're paying a visit to Nabal!"

Now you see the problem, don't you? Just before this event, in 1 Samuel 24, David had experienced a tremendous victory in showing tenderness and love toward his enemy. And he is going to show it again in chapter 26, when he has another opportunity to take Saul's life. But sandwiched between chapters 24 and 26, is chapter 25.

The contrast is obvious. In chapters 24 and 26, David is the restrainer; he will not harm Saul himself or permit his men to do so. In chapter 25, David has to be restrained; he and all his men are bent on spilling the blood of Nabal, because of the Beast's outrageous insults. It was as if Nabal's crassness provoked a similar crassness in David.

Do you see the inconsistency? David refuses to harm the anointed king but is perfectly willing to liquidate a private citizen.

We are seeing something here in David that we haven't considered before. David can be dangerous! He is to be feared! And the people around him know it. He is leading a group of tough men who can just as easily cut your throat as look at you. David has a dark side that can show mercy in one moment and take revenge the next.

And the truth is—so do we.

• • •

There is something inside of us that can show tenderness and patience to an adversary in one instance and can tear into a friend the next. And the line is usually crossed when it has something to do with an assault on our self-image or a bruised ego.

When we are treated with disgrace and disdain, or when we are embarrassed and humiliated, it is very easy to become defensive and to lash out in self-protection. Especially with someone we consider to be a lesser human being to begin with. And the ease with which we are able to cross the line at times can be frightening!

That's what happened to David. His ego was bruised, and he lost his temper. David lost all sense of his identity as the Lord's anointed. He was on the verge of becoming another Saul, out to get rid of anyone threatening his status and role. He realized how easy it is to be a beauty in one instance and a beast in another.

Fortunately for David, Nabal had not only an intelligent wife but also an observant servant. The servant knew what David was capable of. And he knew he couldn't talk any sense into Nabal, because fools don't listen to advice. And so instead he went to Abigail.

He told Abigail how Nabal had been his usual crabby self and vented his spleen on David's servants. He also said that David was furious and on his way to settle the score.

We learn three important lessons from Abigail's response.

• • •

The Power of God's Restraining Providence

As soon as Abigail heard what had happened, she immediately went into action. In fifteen minutes she organized a full-scale catering service: dinner on a donkey for six hundred men!

She sent out the food first (good advice, ladies—if you want to put a man in a better mood, a good dinner always helps!), and then she followed on her donkey to go out and meet David. Now that was a pretty risky thing to do. Given the hostile intentions of David, and the meanness of her husband, she was putting herself on the line. But she was acting and speaking for God, and she put that ahead of her personal safety.

When Abigail reached David's lynch mob, she jumped off her donkey and fell on her knees before David. The Bible says, "A gentle answer turns away wrath" (Prov. 15:1). She knew what she was doing.

The first thing she did was to take the blame for the whole situation. She accepted Nabal's wrongdoing on herself and asked for David's forgiveness.

She said, "I'm sorry for all that's happened today. Nabal is an idiot! But don't stoop to his level. One fool is enough in this story. Don't forget that you are in God's hands, David. Do you remember how God was with you when you fought Goliath? Do you remember the ways God has protected you against Saul? You're doing God's work, and God is fighting your battles for you. But the moment you try and take matters into your own hands, it ceases to be God's battle, and it becomes yours. As long as you're doing things God's way he will watch over your life" (1 Sam. 25:24-26, author's paraphrase).

Her words were like a healing balm to David's enraged spirit and wounded pride. He was within a whisker of tarnishing his future kingdom with a stain that he could never overcome. And he would have lived with that blot on his royal record for the rest of his life. But Abigail intervened. More accurately, God intervened through Abigail. Notice what Abigail said to David: "The LORD has kept you from bloodshed and from avenging yourself with your own hands" (v. 26).

Providence is God's unseen hand that moves in events and the lives of people to guide our paths and, when necessary, to stop us in our tracks and prevent us from making a mess out of our lives. Sometimes the things we think are roadblocks in our way turn out to be way stations of mercy. Sometimes the things we think are hindrances to our plans turn out to be safety nets of kindness. Thank God for his restraining providence that protects us from ourselves!

Most sin is committed with a very short view in mind. We often respond to our passion in the moment and our gratification for the now. Rarely do we see the long-term consequences of our actions. People who don't consider the future repercussions of what they do in the heat of the moment are called fools!

Abigail's words of warning were God's restraining providence that helped David recognize how his vengefulness would have put his own future at risk. God sent Abigail to help David see the "later."

When David eventually became king, he distanced himself from people who could remind him of the "later." David had no one to intervene with Bathsheba, and he had a train wreck. All he could see was the now.

God won't force us to respond to his wake-up calls. We still have a choice to make when God intervenes in our lives. But our decision to respond to or ignore his intervention doesn't change the fact that God faithfully comes to us by his grace. His restraining and keeping providence can protect us from falling![3]

● ● ●

Beauty Points Us Back to God

There is a long tradition in the Christian life of honoring beauty as a witness to God.[4] In the presence of the beautiful, we have an entrée to the "beauty of the Lord."[5] We see that beauty in creation: mountains and oceans, stars and storms, birds and flowers. We see that beauty in art, music, poetry, and architecture. But most often we see it in a human life that lives in such a way that the beauty of the Lord comes shining through.[6]

It's called the beauty of holiness. It was Abigail's beauty that put David in touch again with the beauty of the Lord that had nearly been obliterated in his vengeance—his obsessed, honor-defending, out-for-blood rampage against Nabal.

That happens to all of us. No one is exempt. Someone offends us, crosses us, or doesn't give us what we want. Our self-importance flares up, and we're off to do something about it—usually off to do something about it armed with righteous indignation. Wrapped up in ourselves, we're angry and ready to defend our honor. We're off to avenge hurt feelings and bruised self-images. We say, "We'll get even, get them back, show them a thing or two."

But suddenly we're stopped in our tracks by something beautiful—a sleeping child, an understanding friend, a singing bird, a magenta sunset, an Abigail. God shines through and we find ourselves confronted with something quite other than what we're feeling and doing. And we suddenly realize that *we* are quite other than what we're feeling and doing.

The David whom we are used to seeing as "full of God" was, at that moment, full of himself. David has been described as beautiful before, but there is no sign of that beauty now. However, through "beautiful" Abigail, David is called back to what God is doing in his life. Abigail recovers a vision of God for David. She points him back to his God-ordained purpose.

• • •

God Brings People to Stand in the Gap

People who stand in the gap are called peacemakers. Jesus said, "Blessed are the peacemakers, for they will be called children of God" (Matt. 5:9). Peacemakers strive to move us to the sacred intersection where our will is reconciled with God's will.

Most of us want that kind of peace in our world. Indeed, most of us pray for it. But we want it to be done by somebody else. It is much more difficult to rush, like Abigail, into the brokenness of daily life, where fools provoke violence, and stand in the gap for God and his people. We want someone else to stand in the gap!

Abigail doesn't wait for someone else. Someone else may be too late. She intervenes. She intercedes. And the beauty of her holiness stops angry, hell-bent David in his tracks. And she brings peace.

There are plenty of fools in this world, and they push us to our breaking point. But no sooner do we set out for personal justice than we enter into the same foolish wickedness that we're determined to get rid of.

David had been living as God's anointed and blessed person, and it nearly got away from him as he pursued his puny, small-minded revenge. Had it not been for Abigail, David would have done in both Nabal and himself. David is free of vengeance, hate, and remorse because Abigail stood in the gap. She saved his life and his future.

• • •

I heard the story of two men who grew up best friends. Though Jim was a little older than Philip, and often assumed the role of leader, they did everything together. They even went to high school and college together. After college, they decided to join the Army.

By a unique series of circumstances they were sent to Germany together, where they fought side by side in World War II. During a fierce battle, amid heavy gunfire, bombing, and hand-to-hand combat, they were given the command to retreat. As the men were running back, Jim noticed that Philip had not returned with the others. Panic gripped his heart. Jim knew if Philip was not back in another minute or two that he wouldn't make it.

Jim begged his commanding officer to let him go after his friend, but the officer denied the request, saying it would be suicide. Risking his own life, Jim disobeyed the order and went after Philip. His heart pounding, he ran into the gunfire, calling out Philip's name.

A short time later, his platoon saw him hobbling across the field carrying a limp body in his arms. Jim's commanding officer reprimanded him, shouting that it was a foolish waste of time and an outrageous risk. "Your friend is dead, and there was nothing you could do."

"No sir, you're wrong," Jim replied. "I got there just in time. Before he died, his last words were, 'I knew you would come.'"

An early Christian named James writes, "My dear brothers and sisters, if someone among you wanders away from the truth and is brought back, you can be sure that whoever brings the sinner back will save that person from death and bring about the forgiveness of many sins" (James 5:19-20, NLT).

Standing in the gap can be risky business. But in God's faithfulness, someone has stood in the gap for you. Are you willing to stand in the gap for someone else?

• • •

This story ends in a surprising way. Nabal parties all night and goes to bed drunk. The next morning, Abigail tells him what had happened the day before, and the Beast has a stroke on the spot. The Bible says God struck Nabal dead! This is a serious news flash to all fools! "The fool says in his heart, 'There is no God'" (Ps. 14:1), but here God has struck the heart of the fool.

David is no fool! The last thing Abigail said to David that day on the road was, "Remember me when God keeps his promise to you" (1 Sam. 25:31, author's paraphrase). He does not forget, and he sends for Abigail to be his wife.

The next time you are tempted by a fool, look for God's beauty in the world. And don't be surprised if God's restraining providence turns out to be someone standing in the gap for you.

11

THE SOUND OF
FINE SILENCE

1 KINGS 19

Silence is God's first language;
everything else is a poor translation.
–Thomas Keating[1]

I LIKE how my friend Scott defines solitude. He says, "Solitude is the practice of being absent from other people and other things in order to be present with God."[2]

In solitude we learn to wait on the Lord and to pray, "I am here to be changed into whatever you like."

When I think about the power of solitude, I think about Elijah. Elijah was a prophet of God.

Elijah was no spiritual weakling. He was a mighty man of God. He prayed that it wouldn't rain for three years, and it didn't. He raised a widow's son back to life. He faced down kings and queens against great odds. God sent birds to bring him bread and meat.

He was sent to confront the idolatry of the people of Israel and to denounce Baal worship.

On one occasion, he had a showdown with the prophets of Baal on Mount Carmel.[3] It was 450 bad guys against 1 prophet of God. All the people of Israel were invited. Both sides slaughtered and prepared a bull for a sacrifice. But instead of lighting a fire for the sacrifice, the contest was to see who was serving the real God. Which deity would answer by fire?

The bad guys went first. The priests of Baal danced around their sacrifice, calling on the name of their god. They shouted, "Baal, answer us!" (1 Kings 18:26). To their credit, they were persistent. They did this from morning until noon.

Elijah couldn't help himself. He started prophet trash-talking. And he laid it on thick: "Maybe your god's asleep. Maybe he's on vacation. Maybe you should shout a little louder!" (v. 27, author's paraphrase).[4]

This taunting only threw the prophets of Baal into more of a frenzy. They began screaming even louder and cut themselves with knives and spears to show Baal how serious they really were. They did this until evening time.

Finally, Elijah said, "If you guys are through, it's my turn now." Then, just to be sure no one would think that perhaps Baal had started to heat things up, and that the one true God needed help, he told the people to pour water over his sacrifice and soak the wood. In fact, he made them do it three times until, the Bible says, water was pouring off of the sacrifice and down into the trench. Then Elijah looked up to heaven and prayed a prayer that went something like this: "Show them who the real God is!"

Zap! Fire fell from heaven and not only consumed the sacrifice but even dried up all the water. The people were in awe. They said, "The LORD—he is God!" (v. 39). Then they killed all the prophets of Baal right on the spot.

Elijah immediately sent a message to the corrupt King Ahab: "You better get in your chariot and ride down this mountain, because there's a storm a-coming!"

Ahab replied, "It hasn't rained here for three years."

Elijah said, "That's because I prayed that it wouldn't. Now I'm praying that it will."

Suddenly the power of the Lord came upon Elijah and gave him supernatural strength. And in a dramatic scene worthy of the Summer Olympics, Elijah raced all the way down the mountain in front of the king's chariot, while the Lord raced behind him on a thundercloud.

I'm telling you that Elijah was no spiritual weakling!

Meanwhile, King Ahab went back to the palace and told his wife what had happened. Her name was Jezebel, and she was an evil queen. Not only was she evil, but she also wore the pants in the family. When she told Ahab to jump, he said, "How high?"

Jezebel was extremely upset at what had happened. You didn't want to get Jezebel upset. She ordered a hit on Elijah's life. Then she sent a message to Elijah: "You better watch your back, because I'm coming to get you. In twenty-four hours, you're going to be just as dead as the prophets of Baal."

For some reason, this really got to Elijah. We have no record of him acting in fear before, but this time he did.

He ran for his life—into the desert.

He ran for so long and so far that he finally fell down absolutely exhausted. He crawled up underneath a broom tree and started praying: "Lord, I've had about all I can take. I'm completely fried. I'm a miserable prophet, better dead than alive. So please, just take my life!"

● ● ●

Now let's stop. This is crazy.

One minute Elijah is running in front of a chariot; the next minute he's running for his life in the wilderness. One minute he's going toe-to-toe with 450 prophets; the next minute he wants to throw in the towel and give up on life.

What's going on?

He's tired.

He is emotionally and physically drained. He is completely frazzled, depressed, and has lost his focus. And at the moment, life seems bigger than God.

Have you ever felt that way? Ever lost your focus? Ever feel as though life is bigger than God?

I love what God does for Elijah.

God doesn't scold him: "Boy, you need to go read your Bible! If you would, you'd find out that Jezebel isn't in control. I am!"

God doesn't shame him: "What do I have to do to prove myself to you? I fed you with birds. I helped you raise someone from the dead. I sent fire from heaven. I sent rain in the drought. When you were completely outnumbered, I had your back. You need to get it together!"

No, God says, "Elijah, you need a nap. You're tired. You're worn out. You need some sleep."

Isn't that great? Sleep is God's gift to Elijah.

There's a difference between spiritual failure and physical and emotional exhaustion. But when you're tired and worn out, it's hard to be spiritually focused, much less focused on anything else in your life.

● ● ●

As a pastor I would occasionally have young mothers with small children come to me and say, "Pastor David, I think I'm losing it. I'm ready to climb the walls. I'm not very loving. I've got a short fuse. I'm a terrible mom. I don't think Jesus loves me anymore."

I would usually say, "You're not a bad person. You need some sleep! You need to do a 'nap trade-off' with your friends. You can watch *their* kids so they can get a long nap, and then they can watch *your* kids so you can get a long nap."

I have a good friend who was able to take a two-week course in spiritual formation from Dallas Willard. He was there with a group of twenty pastors. The first day of class, Dallas said, "This is your assignment for tonight. I want all of you to go to bed at 9:00 p.m. And then I don't want you to get up until 7:00 a.m. As hard as it may be, I want you to try and get ten hours of sleep tonight. Some of you haven't had a good night's sleep in so long you've forgotten what it feels like. But you can't be spiritually focused and sleep deprived. Get some rest and then you'll be ready for this class."

Hmmmm? Sleep? Spiritually forming?

· · ·

God is so serious about Elijah getting some rest that he even sends an angel to be sure he gets, not one, but *two* long naps. After the first nap, the Lord wakes up Elijah and says, "That was Spiritual Formation 101—now it's time for Spiritual Formation 201. You need to eat something." Elijah turns around, and there is hot bread fresh out of the oven plus a big glass of cold water.

You know, things are pretty basic with God. When you're tired, he wants you to sleep. When you're hungry, he wants you to eat. Why? Because he knows we're not just spiritual beings. We are complex organisms that depend on the intricate balance between the physical, emotional, and spiritual. But sometimes our hurried lives rob us of the rhythms of adequate rest and proper nutrition, and then we wonder why we feel so out of kilter.

We think we have so much to do and so little time to do it. God rescues us from hurry sickness. He steps in and says, "Yes, those things are important, but first you need to slow down. You're tired. Everything's out of whack. You can't think straight. You've lost your perspective. Let me 'unhurry' you so that I can have your undivided attention."

· · ·

There's a story in the Gospels that recounts a time when Jesus and his disciples had been through a long stretch of ongoing ministry work. Jesus knows that his disciples are beginning to wear down. Jesus can see the frazzled look on their faces.

> Then, because so many people were coming and going that they did not even have a chance to eat, he said to them,

"Come with me by yourselves to a quiet place and get some rest." (Mark 6:31)

I've noticed some people wear their busyness like a badge of honor (especially pastors). It's as though they believe when they die, God is going to look at them and say, "What a great life you've had! You were even too busy to eat. And look at those black circles under your eyes. Well done good and faithful servant!"

That's not how it works! Jesus knows that. He knows we have our limits. He knows we need balance. That's why he says: "Come with me by yourselves to a quiet place and get some rest" (v. 31).

That's what God said to Elijah too. First Kings 19:7 says, "Get up and eat, for the journey is too much for you." God knows what we can handle. He knows what we need to stay balanced and function at optimal levels.

• • •

After a couple of long naps and some good food, Elijah is thinking better. He is now ready for some solitude with God. Elijah decides to go to Mount Horeb. That's significant for two reasons.

First of all, Mount Horeb is another name for Mount Sinai, which happened to be the mountain where God gave Moses the Ten Commandments. It's also significant because guess how long it took Elijah to get there? Forty days and forty nights—the same length of time that Moses had spent with God on the mountain. Moses' time alone with God had filled him with such spiritual strength that when he came down from the mountain, his face was glowing. No wonder Elijah wanted to go to Mount Horeb.

• • •

Solitude is an interesting thing. Solitude *without* God is destructive. That's why our prison systems use solitary confinement as a form of punishment. Solitude is used to break people down because relational interaction is needed to prop up a broken person. If you take that away, it's like taking away the only scaffolding of support they have.

Solitude, apart from God, breaks us down.

Conversely, solitude *with* God builds us up. It doesn't weaken us—it gives us inner strength and peace and helps us find our bearings.

Again, Jesus taught us that. Following his baptism, and at the very beginning of his public ministry, we are told that the Spirit *led* Jesus into the wilderness, and there he was tempted by the devil.[5]

Now some people think that this was Jesus at his weakest point. "Well, look," they say, "Jesus was starving and all alone out there in the middle of nowhere with no one to help him. No wonder the devil attacked him." But I don't see it that way. The place of solitude alone with God was actually an incredible place of *strengthening* for Jesus. That's why the Spirit led him there to begin with—to put Jesus in a place of utmost inner strength for his ultimate temptations.

Think about it.

Do you think Satan would have left Jesus alone if he had *not* gone into the wilderness?

Would Jesus have faced any temptations if he had not been in solitude?

Of course! But Jesus had been in the solitary presence of God, fasting and praying, for more than a month (forty days to be exact) before Satan was allowed to approach him. Jesus would have been at the pinnacle of his spiritual strength. Only *then* was Satan allowed to throw his worst at Jesus.

Solitude with God became Jesus' source of inner strength and basis of power. No wonder Luke tells us, "When the devil had finished all this tempting, he left him until an *opportune* time" (Luke 4:13, emphasis added).

No wonder Jesus continued to practice solitude throughout his life. The Gospels mention over forty times that Jesus spent time alone with his Father. Luke tells us, "Jesus *often* withdrew to lonely places and prayed" (5:16, emphasis added). That's how serious Jesus was about the practice of solitude. He didn't do it because he was bored. He didn't do it because he wasn't busy. He did it because he knew it was the place to draw his strength.

What would happen if every Christian actually did that? What if every Christian said, "I'm going to get away and just be with God on a regular basis." What if that became our standard practice— maybe not for forty days at a time—but long enough and frequent enough to get our heads and hearts unhurried in God's presence?

What would happen?

● ● ●

After forty days, Elijah reached Mount Horeb. He went into a cave and spent the night.

I love this next part. The text says, "And the word of the LORD came to him" (1 Kings 19:9). Do you know what that says to me?

When we take the time to meet God in solitude, God will speak to us.

God said, "What are you doing here, Elijah?" (v. 9).

Elijah doesn't try and pretend he's doing better than he is. He is totally honest before God. He speaks what is in his heart. Here is my paraphrase of Elijah's response to God: "I'm mad! I'm scared! What are you going to do to help me?"

Elijah had escaped the outer noise, but he hadn't escaped the inner noise. Elijah was finally alone with God, but he wasn't quiet. Things were very loud inside. There was still fear, anxiety, and insecurity. He had slowed his body down, but he had not yet listened.

"Get ready, Elijah." God said, "For the Lord is about to pass by" (v. 11).

What happened next is powerful.

An incredible wind began blowing so forcefully that the mountain began to rip apart. Rocks were just being shattered and ripped to pieces. And Elijah listened hard. But he couldn't hear God, because "the Lord was not in the wind" (v. 11).

That was followed by a powerful earthquake that shook the ground. And Elijah listened hard. But he could not hear God, because "the Lord was not in the earthquake" (v. 11).

Then there came a raging fire, and the heat was intense. And Elijah listened hard. But he could not hear God, because "the Lord was not in the fire" (v. 12). Remember, not long before this, God was in the fire and the storm on Mount Carmel. But he was not found there on Mount Horeb.

Suddenly, everything became very still. It was an eerie calm. You know that eerie calm that comes right before an Oklahoma tornado is about to hit? It was that kind of stillness. And Elijah heard something.

The Hebrew words literally say that there was a "sound of fine silence" (see v. 12). The King James Version says that there was a "still small voice." The *New International Version* and the *New Living Translation* say that there was a "gentle whisper." The *New Revised Standard Version* is as close as any to the original language; it says that there was a "sound of sheer silence." And in this silence, Elijah heard something.

God was not in the storm, the earthquake, or the fire, but God was here in this quiet stillness.

Elijah knows he is standing on holy ground. Just as Moses had met God in a burning bush, now Elijah meets God through a "sound of fine silence." He doesn't take off his shoes as Moses did, but in an act of submission, he covers his face with his cloak and steps out of the cave.

The Lord asks for a second time, "What are you doing here, Elijah?" (v. 13).

Elijah hardly knows what to say. He repeats the same thing to the Lord now that he did before. Only this time I think it is different. These are just my thoughts, but I think that earlier, Elijah's response was raw. It was full of passion, emotion, and frustration. But this time I think Elijah has tears in his eyes. I hear a soft voice. I see a quivering lip. Not out of fear, but of renewed tenderness and awe in God's presence.

I think he was saying: "Lord, I still don't understand what has happened. I still have the same feelings I did before. But I *know* you are with me."

In that moment of silence and solitude, God spoke words of real comfort and renewed direction to Elijah. Elijah's strength was replenished, and he left Mount Horeb in the power of the Spirit.

● ● ●

We learn an important lesson in this story about the practice of solitude. God's voice is heard most clearly, not in loud, dramatic commotion, but in quiet and solitude. Nor is God's voice heard in the incessant noise and constant rush of the hurried pace of life, but in the "sound of fine silence."

One of my friends once heard a Catholic nun say, "If you're look-ing for God—God is in the pause." It was in the pause when God finally got Elijah's full attention.

In the pause Elijah found his balance again. No wonder David wrote, "He makes me lie down in green pastures, he leads me beside quiet waters, he *refreshes* my soul" (Ps. 23:2-3, emphasis added).

Please don't misunderstand my point. I believe that folks should be reading their Bibles, going to church, and being involved in ministry. But if Bible reading, going to church, and being in-volved in ministry were enough to really change a person, then there ought to be more conclusive evidence that it works. The problem is that a lot of religious folks are routinely doing those things and not really being changed.

Reading ten Bible verses a day is good, but it's not magic either. It has to get down deep in our souls and take root. Bullet prayers fired up on the run are unloading, and we feel better for praying them, but are they really changing us?

There is no such thing as microwave maturity. The writer Henri Nouwen wrote, "Solitude is the furnace of transformation. Without solitude we remain victims of our society and continue to be entangled in the illusions of the false self."[6] The only real and lasting change happens by lingering in the presence of God.

Jesus told a parable that illustrated how people receive the Word of God. For some, their heart soil is too shallow, too hard, or too entangled in other affairs, and the Word has no real effect. That's where solitude and silence can really help us. They are the container vessels for other spiritual practices. They sufficiently "unhurry" us and disengage us from our insane habits long enough to allow the other practices of prayer, study, and fasting to have their full impact.

That is the power of the "sound of fine silence." It will help us find our way. The payoff is inner strength, resilient joy, and God's peace.

WE COULDN'T STOP CRYING

NEHEMIAH 8:1-12

Joy is the serious business of heaven.
–C. S. Lewis[1]

NEHEMIAH and a committed group of Jewish exiles accomplished far more than they ever imagined possible. For that matter, they accomplished more than *anyone* had imagined. There were major obstacles to overcome and intense opposition, both internally and externally, but with the help of the Lord, it really happened. The broken-down walls of Jerusalem were rebuilt in an astounding fifty-two days.

What do you do when you come to a milestone moment of that magnitude? You throw a party!

It was the seventh month in the Jewish calendar. The Israelites came from all of the surrounding towns and villages to celebrate what God had done through them. The city of Jerusalem was jam-packed. Everyone assembled in one of the city squares. It was almost dawn.

Ezra the scribe was there. Several years before, Ezra had led a small group of exiles to rebuild the temple. Just as the sun began to peek over the horizon, he walked up onto the platform that had been built for the occasion and turned and faced all the people. In his hand was a scroll of the law of Moses.

A hush fell over the crowd as Ezra lifted the book. When he opened the book, all the people stood to their feet. It was a high and holy moment. When Ezra held up the book, the crowd erupted in one voice with a shout that could be heard a mile away.

They began to praise the Lord, the great God who had redeemed them and given them strength to complete their task. They all shouted, "Amen! Amen!" (Neh. 8:6), meaning, "We agree; may it be so!" Then they all "bowed down and worshiped the LORD with their faces to the ground" (v. 6).

Then, starting at the beginning, Ezra began to read from the Law.[2] The people stood to their feet again and remained standing as long as he read.[3]

Now when we hear the word "law," we tend to think in negative ways. We think of something that is harsh, demanding, and legalistic. But not these people. For them, the Law revealed a gracious God who had invited them into a covenant relationship. It was about how God, for no other reason than sheer love and pure grace, had said to them, "You will be my holy people, and I will reveal my purpose for creation through you."

Keep in mind that it had been a very long time since they had been able to worship together as a people. For the vast majority, this gathering might have even been their first experience.

Not only that, they had not *read* or *heard* the Word of God in the holy city of Jerusalem for over one hundred years. And many had never heard the Word read at all.

As Ezra read, they heard about God creating the world in all its splendor and beauty.

They heard about the failings of humanity and that God would not give up on them.

They heard that God redeemed his people from slavery in Egypt.

They heard that God made a covenant with his people and gave them the words of life.

They remembered that God brought their ancestors to the Promised Land many years before and that he had brought them back again from Babylon.

From daybreak until noon, they stood and listened to the Word. It was a six-hour sermon!

The Levites explained the meaning of the words the people were hearing, and as the people listened attentively, their hearts were captured by the magnitude of this moment.

It was such a powerful moment, and the words were so beautiful, that when they realized how far they had fallen short, the people began to weep.

And they couldn't stop crying.

● ● ●

Why were they crying? Was it for joy or sadness?

Sometimes people cry because loss and grief overwhelm them. Sometimes people cry bitter tears of remorse and regret. Sometimes people cry because they have so much joy that normal emotions won't do, and tears are the only way to express it.

So why were the people crying?

On the one hand, their hearts were broken because they had lost their way, and the broken-down walls of Jerusalem were symbolic of their own broken-down lives. They had *not* been faithful to God, and it broke their hearts. This is called *conviction*.

But on the other hand, they were also weeping for joy at the reminder of who they were and to whom they belonged. They were people called Jews, people of the book, responsible to and loved by the living God. This is called *confirmation*.

The truth is, every time God's Word is read, it brings one or both of those responses. Sometimes the Word confirms in us that we are walking in paths of righteousness and encourages us to stay the course. Sometimes the Word convicts us—makes us aware that we have strayed from the path—and calls us back.

But either way, it is all grace, because how else would we know?

● ● ●

No wonder the people couldn't stop crying. This book contained God's words of life to them; a beautiful gift of grace.

When Nehemiah and Ezra saw the people weeping, they said, "This day is holy to the LORD your God. Do not mourn or weep" (Neh. 8:9).

Then Nehemiah said a profound thing: "Go and enjoy choice food and sweet drinks, and send some to those who have nothing prepared. This day is holy to our Lord. Do not grieve, for the joy of the LORD is your strength" (v. 10).

I love this verse for three reasons.

I love it because the Bible explicitly says that we don't have to drink Diet Coke and eat broccoli. We can swig A&W Root Beer and chow down on onion rings. We can drink sweet drinks and enjoy choice food.

I also love this verse because whatever celebration looks like for the people of God, it always includes those who have less. While we are celebrating, we are called to think about those who have nothing prepared and invite them to the table. That has something to do with compassion for the needy and oppressed.

And I love this verse because it reminds us that to declare a day "holy [or sacred] to our LORD" (v. 10) means—it's party time! It's a time for feasting, not fasting! It's a time for rejoicing, not grieving!

What do you do on a day holy and sacred to the Lord? You party!

There is a time for weeping, and the people will weep and confess their sins before God in the chapters ahead. There is a time and place for that. But Nehemiah wants to be clear: the bottom line is not our brokenness; it is the good news that God is our God and that our God loves us.

"The joy of the LORD is your strength" (v. 10). So, Nehemiah says, do some things that bring you joy. Go and eat—but not just any food—choice food. Go and drink—but not just any drinks— sweet drinks.

Do some things that bring you joy. And don't forget to share some of it with the folks who have nothing, because this is what God's new community is about.

Why is celebration and joy so important?

• • •

There are more than sixty references in Scripture that pertain to celebration. And almost without exception, they are divine imperatives—commands from God to go party!

For example, in the Hebrew Scriptures[4] God mandated no fewer than twelve annual feasts and festivals that his people were to participate in. That's about one per month. Several of these feasts and festivals lasted for a full seven days. That's about one week per month. These festive occasions included the Feast of the Passover, the Feast of Weeks, and the Feast of Tabernacles.

What did the people do during those feasts and festivals? They worshipped God and brought some offerings in the mornings. But the rest of the afternoon was spent throwing a communal party (again, mandated by God).

And these were not quiet, serene, dignified, highfalutin little parties where you drink tea with your pinky in the air. These were raucous, shout-at-the-top-of-your-lungs, dance-in-the-streets, weeklong shindigs, with a lot of great food, great drink, and great fellowship—and laughter—a lot of laughter.

There was no work allowed, no checking emails on your iPhone, no trading on the stock market. Just celebrating!

It was almost as though their heavenly Father were saying, "I want you kids to go on out and have a good time. I'm not asking you—I'm telling you! Just go out and blow the doors off. Laugh until your sides hurt."

Why? Because "the joy of the LORD is your strength" (Neh. 8:10)! And that's the Old Testament.

Jesus comes along and doesn't miss a beat.

• • •

It has always fascinated me that Jesus' very first recorded miracle wasn't healing someone who was sick, forgiving someone's sins, or raising someone from the dead.

Do you remember what Jesus' first miracle was? Saving a party on the brink of ruin. It's true. He turned water into wine at a wedding feast (see John 2).

Now in those days a wedding feast wasn't just drinking orange sherbet punch and munching on pastel breath mints. They were wildly fun celebrations with, once again, a lot of choice-food eating, sweet-drink drinking, intergenerational dancing, and rip-roaring laughter. Are you starting to see a pattern?

These wedding feasts would often go on for days. On this particular occasion, Jesus was attending the wedding feast, and the host of the party ran out of "sweet drink." Now you would think that a religious leader, like Jesus, would say that's a good thing. They ran out of wine while people were still able to stand. But apparently Jesus thought the party should go on.

And so out of all the inaugural miracles he could have done—and Jesus undoubtedly knew that this was going to be recorded as the first—he decided to save the party.

John tells us that Jesus took six stone jars[5] and had them filled to the brim with water. He then rolled up his sleeves and turned the water into wine.

I recently heard someone calculate how much wine we are talking about here.[6] Conservatively speaking, this would roughly be equivalent to Jesus making over six hundred bottles of wine today. I think he may have exceeded the need.[7]

Not only that, according to John, after tasting the new wine, the wedding's master of ceremonies commented that the bridegroom had saved the best wine for last. Such an occurrence would have been highly unusual considering that after the guests were thoroughly loosened up, they wouldn't have cared if it had been cherry Kool-Aid.

That's a very interesting first miracle!

Throughout the remainder of his public ministry, Jesus proceeded to attend so many celebrations and feasts that some of the more uptight religious folks actually began to accuse him of liking parties too much.

One time a group of folks were very concerned that Jesus' disciples didn't engage more often in serious religious practices such as fasting. Jesus responded (my paraphrase), "You don't get chintzy when it's time to celebrate. Someday when the bridegroom is gone, they'll fast. But right now, it's party time."[8]

The Pharisees of the day loathed that perspective. They thought Jesus was too irreverent, too frivolous, too irresponsible, and a threat to religious order and decency. It actually got to the point that they started blogging about Jesus and accused him of being a drunkard and a glutton.[9]

It wasn't true, of course. It was a false accusation. Jesus was never immoral or unrighteous in anything he did. But it was their paranoid way of saying, "You know, for a religious guy you like parties way too much!"

Jesus' lifestyle philosophy drove them completely nuts! They screeched, "Stop all that celebrating! Stop all that singing! Stop all that dancing! Stop all that laughing! And most of all, stop making religion fun!"

"Stop it! Stop it! Stop it!"

But he wouldn't. Indeed, he couldn't. Because joy, utter and complete joy, was a sign of the in-breaking kingdom of God. Whenever Jesus talked about the kingdom, he would often use the imagery of a great banquet with all kinds of joy-filled people sitting around a table with limitless amounts of food, drink, laughter, and carrying-on.

That's our God. If you hear Jesus talk about it long enough, you begin to get the idea that our God is looking for just about any excuse to fire up the barbecue and invite the neighborhood over.

Whenever someone gets saved, heaven throws a party. When a lost sheep is found, the shepherd does a dance. When a lost son comes home, his dad sprints down the road.

It's as if the nature of the kingdom is all about celebration, joy, and laughter, because that's the heart of the God of the kingdom. Oh, for now we have our fair share of death, mourning, crying, and pain. It's part of a fallen world. But don't get used to it, because you won't find any of that in heaven.

Sometimes someone will ask me, "What will be in heaven? What will we do in heaven?" Among many answers I could give, the life of Jesus tells us at least this much.

Do you know what we'll find in heaven? Joy.

Do you know what we'll do in heaven? Celebrate.

Do you know what we'll hear in heaven? Laughter.

● ● ●

Laughter is the sound of heaven.

I have had the delightful privilege of spending my whole life with people who like to laugh. My dad had the charming habit of telling jokes that he could never finish. That's because right in the middle of telling the joke, he would start thinking about the punch line and get so tickled he couldn't get it out. I don't remember him ever getting to the finish line of a joke without cracking himself up so much that anyone listening couldn't help but start laughing too!

When I was a kid, I used to buy those Weekly Reader joke books. They had the corniest jokes imaginable, most of them having something to do with pickles ("Did you hear the one about the pickle and the astronaut . . . ?"). But I would buy them anyway just so I could read those jokes to my dad over and over while he laughed until tears were running down his face.[10]

What a gift.

My wife is a laugher. If you are in a crowded room, with people talking and carrying on, when Christi starts laughing, everyone in the room knows *who* is laughing. I have always loved that about her!

One night we were sitting on our back patio with some friends, and we were telling funny stories. Christi was in rare form, laughing heartily and having a lot of fun. Suddenly my cell phone rang. It was a call from our friends Laine and Susan, who lived on the other side of the lake: "We can't believe it! We were sitting here in our backyard and heard Christi laughing. We had to call!"

They were across the lake! I think that's exquisite!

I wish I could be more like that. Sometimes I'm too serious. I wish I could be a little more like my friend Kendall.

Kendall is, and always has been, one funny guy. A long time ago we were youth pastors together on the same district. We went to a youth conference together in Dallas. On the way home, our airplane had to travel through a major thunderstorm. I have flown hundreds of flights since, but it is still one of the scariest plane rides I've ever experienced. The plane was literally bucking up and down, back and forth. We honestly didn't know if we were going to make it.

You can tell a lot about a person when he or she is about to die. Your true self comes out.

As we were bouncing up and down in the plane, I got very quiet. My upper lip started sweating, and I was clutching the armrests with a white-knuckled death grip.

Kendall wasn't sweating or clutching. He just started laughing, hysterically and loudly, laughing—at death. I always thought that meant Kendall was closer to the Lord than I was. But it broke the ice.

The whole plane started laughing with Kendall, including the guy with the sweaty lip and death grip.

• • •

When I think of Jesus, I don't see an ultraserious, frown-on-the-face, stiff-upper-lip, scolding-type person whose pants are too tight.

That's what the Pharisees were about. Their mind-set was, "If it's fun, it can't be spiritual. If it's funny, it must be sacrilegious. If it's joyful, it must be shallow."

They were like the elder brother in the parable of the prodigal son. They were so busy keeping all the rules, figuring the cost of the homecoming shindig, and mulling over why everybody should be so happy while they were so miserable that they didn't have time to sit down and just enjoy the party.

When I think of Jesus, I see someone who is the life of the party. I see him sitting in the center of a circle, with a lot of people standing around him, while he jokes, winks, and throws back his head and gives a big belly laugh.

Jesus was fun! Why else would the same folks who hated being around uptight, legalistic people love spending time with Jesus? Why else did kids like being with him? Because he was fun to be around!

It didn't mean he crossed the line. It didn't mean he was ever crass. It didn't mean he told oversexualized jokes and made fun of people to get a laugh. Of course not!

But he knew something we Christians sometimes forget: "The joy of the LORD is [our] strength" (Neh. 8:10). Maybe that's why Jesus also said, "I want *my* joy to be in you so that *your* joy may be complete" (John 15:11, author's paraphrase).

● ● ●

How did we ever get the idea that being a Christian was a boring, depressing, sad life?

Have we forgotten to play, laugh, dance, and *live*?

Do we believe that the joy of the Lord really is our strength?

• • •

My son, Ben, had a friend he worked with who told him once, "I want to go to hell someday."

Surprised, Ben asked, "Why in the world would you want to do that?"

"Because," his friend said, "I like fast women and fast cars, and I think fast women and fast cars will be there."

Ben responded, "I think you may have the wrong impression of hell."

Mark Buchanan has written a paradigm-busting book called *Your God Is Too Safe*. He writes about this wrong impression of eternal destinations.

> If you think—as popular lore has it—that hell is the party place where you get to slap the backs and tousle the hair of all your pals, drink a Budweiser and dance the hokeypokey with them, you've got your addresses seriously scrambled.
>
> The party's up above!
>
> Down below? Grim, sour solemnity. Long, scowling faces. Endless scolding speeches. Much wagging of the finger, knitting of the brow, quibbling over minor points. Rivalry. Hostility. Envy. The very last place you'll find a party is in hell.[11]

Or to say it another way, the real party is in heaven. Laughter is the sound of heaven, and therefore celebration, at its heart, is a little glimpse of heaven.

Again, as Buchanan so deftly writes,

Celebration is the practice of lifting our eyes from our preoccupation with all the work we have to do and the trouble we're in and the money we owe and the reputation we strive to keep—to lift our eyes from all that and set them on things above. . . . It's the discipline of setting joy before us so that we might throw off everything that hinders and run the race marked out for us—that we might endure and not lose heart and not grow weary.[12]

There will be times of sorrow, sadness, and seriousness in this life. There is no way around it. There are burdens to carry, sins to confess, and relationships to mend. But that's not where our strength comes from. "The joy of the LORD is [our] strength" (Neh. 8:10).

The early Nazarenes, the denomination of which I am a part, understood that. They couldn't stop celebrating! They had the joy of the Lord! Phineas Bresee,[13] the primary founder of the Church of the Nazarene, pastored a church in Los Angeles that was nicknamed the Glory Barn because there was so much singing, shouting, laughing, and carrying on in the worship services.

Some criticized him for it, but it wasn't for show. And it wasn't emotionalism. They had discovered the joy of the Lord, and they couldn't contain themselves. Life just spilled out of them! And that joy was so contagious that people were attracted to them like a moth to the flame.

What if our churches learned to throw parties again?

What if we designated those party times as days holy and sacred to the Lord? (see v. 10).

And what if every celebration included the people on the margins who have lost their laughter?

Nehemiah has done us a great service. He has jogged our collective memory that celebration is the way of the kingdom of God.

And for those of us who couldn't stop crying, he has given us the unadulterated reminder that "the joy of the LORD is [our] strength" (v. 10).

13

IS ANYBODY ELSE UP THERE?

ISAIAH 7:1-16

Never be afraid to trust an
unknown future to a known God.
–Corrie ten Boom[1]

YOU'VE PROBABLY HEARD the story about the man who fell off the cliff but managed to grab a branch and stop his fall. As he hung there, he cried out, "Help! Help! Is anybody up there?"

"I am here," a voice answered.

"Who are you?" yelled the man.

"I am the Lord, and I am here to help you."

"Oh, thank you, Lord! Am I ever glad you're here! I'll do anything you ask me, Lord. Please, just get me out of this predicament!"

"I will help you, but . . . you must let go of the branch."

After a long pause, the man said, "Is anybody else up there?"

• • •

Isaiah 7 opens with the tiny country of Judah facing what appeared to be an insurmountable crisis. There was a desperate man in Judah hanging precariously by a branch who was asking, "Is anybody else up there?"

The united kingdom of Israel that flourished under the reign of King David and King Solomon was no more. There was a major power struggle over who should be the ensuing king, and as a result the kingdom was divided into a northern and a southern kingdom.[2]

The northern kingdom continued to be called Israel (or Ephraim), claiming the majority of Palestine as its territory. Israel named as its capital a city called Samaria. The southern kingdom changed its name to Judah and controlled a tiny plot of land in the southeast corner of Palestine. It was surrounded by the Dead Sea to the east and enemies on every side. Judah called their capital city Jerusalem.

At that time there was a bully on the block named Assyria. Assyria was the most powerful empire in the ancient world in 732 BC, bar none. The Assyrians were formidable, they were dominant, and they had no competition.

Let me put it into perspective. The strength of the Assyrian Empire at that time was more powerful than the United States of America and what was once the Soviet Union—*combined*. And Judah, well, Judah was Rhode Island.

How does that matchup sound? Rhode Island versus the United States and the former Soviet Union combined? That's comparable to a junior high basketball team taking on the NBA All-Stars.

Not exactly a fair fight. Therein was the beginning of the crisis, because being all-world wasn't enough for Assyria. It wanted to be all-universe! And now Assyria had set its greedy eye toward the West.

Oh, and guess who was in the West? Judah and Israel.

Judah was always getting picked on by somebody. Being separated from the northern kingdom only made Judah more vulnerable. But Israel was in a serious predicament as well, because Assyria was on the march and taking no prisoners.

Presuming that multiple armies were better than going solo, Israel decided to form a military alliance with some other countries. It was the ancient version of the United Nations. Israel chose Syria for a partner.

If it sounds complicated, it was. But it was not nearly as prickly as when Israel and Syria decided they needed Judah's help as well. The king of Israel, named Pekah, and the king of Syria, named Rezin, came to the king of Judah and said, "We have a snowball's chance in the Sahara Desert of defeating Assyria unless we work together. The only hope for victory is if we're all on the same team. So get on board."

The king of Judah's name was Ahaz. Ahaz's father, Jotham, was a good king. Ahaz's son, Hezekiah, was considered one of the best kings in Judah's history. Unfortunately, with Ahaz, it skipped a generation; Ahaz was not a good king. Ahaz was a compromising chameleon who had a knack for changing colors to match his environment. He was a politician who would do anything to stay in power, including making all sorts of detrimental agreements and shady deals.

Here's an example of Ahaz's style of leadership: After taking a public opinion poll, he permitted the altars and places of worship of other gods to be established in the country. Judah would eventually become so corrupted during his reign that the temple doors were literally closed. What he hoped was protecting the welfare of Judah was only bringing its demise.

But the one thing Ahaz could do was math. And even Ahaz was smart enough to know that Syria + Israel + Judah *still* did not = Assyria. He knew all that really meant was that now it was New Hampshire, Puerto Rico, and Rhode Island against the United States and the former Soviet Union! King Ahaz wanted nothing to do with any uprising against gargantuan Assyria.

When Israel and Syria heard that Ahaz would not join their ranks, they determined to make Judah pay. They made a decision to combine their forces, conquer Judah, and then replace Ahaz with a king who would be a little more in line with their point of view.

When Ahaz discovered what Israel and Syria were planning to do, he did what all weak kings do in a pickle—he panicked. Knowing that Judah didn't have the military firepower to face down Syria and Israel and that being a puppet king was better than not being king at all, Ahaz, the chameleon king, began to hatch a plan.

He made the decision to call for help. Regrettably, he didn't decide to phone a friend. He called Assyria.

Ahaz called Assyria for two reasons: (1) to rescue Judah from the two countries that were threatening it and (2) because he felt he had no other option. He was willing to make Judah a vassal state, in submission to and under the dominion of Assyria, in return for Assyria's protection. But Ahaz had no idea what that compromise would cost him personally and Judah corporately.

That's where our story picks up.

● ● ●

I love this next part. It just so happened that God knew every-thing that was going on. He knew what Assyria was up to. He knew what Israel and Syria were scheming up. And God knew about the trepidation in Ahaz's heart.

Did you know that nothing is hidden from God? There is no tricking the Almighty. There is no pretending with the Omni-present, Omniscient, and Omnipotent One. In fact, the Bible tells us that God knows our thoughts before we even articulate them.

And because God knew what was going on in Ahaz's heart, God graciously commanded the prophet Isaiah, "Take your son and go to the end of the aqueduct, right there where it feeds into the water supply and bleaching pool" (Isa. 7:3, author's paraphrase).

I love that God gave his prophet specific highway directions to be sure he didn't miss it.[3] And then God gave specific guidance on what to say: "King Ahaz will be there, and I want you to deliver a message to him for me. And here's the message: Calm down! Don't panic! Don't be afraid! Just be still!" (v. 4, author's paraphrase).

And Isaiah obeyed. He traveled to the place God instructed him to go and found Ahaz outside the city gate; Ahaz was doing a fi-nal check on the water supply before the city was attacked. Isaiah delivered his message: "God sent me to tell you to calm down. Don't be afraid of Israel and Syria. They're all smoke and no fire. So God says, don't sweat these guys! And not only that, God says you don't have to sweat Assyria either! And do you want to know why, Ahaz? Because the Sovereign Lord says so—the Sovereign Lord says they will not defeat you!"

178 ● IS ANYBODY ELSE UP THERE?

You see, that's been the problem all along for Ahaz. He made the false assumption that his kingdom would rise and fall on the basis of his achievements, strength, and power. He assumed that the only way to survive was to sell out to the highest bidder. He thought he had to change direction every time the wind blew against him.

But he miscalculated a very important part of the equation—the Sovereign Lord says so!

Ahaz forgot about the power of his God. Judah's capital was Jerusalem. Zion was the holy city of Yahweh—Judah's God. And God had promised his faithfulness to the house of David. Ahaz had forgotten not only *who* he was but also *whose* he was! He was seeking for security in everything except the One who could truly provide it.

And so Isaiah was sent to remind him: "Stop worrying! Calm down! Slow down long enough to remember *whose* you are. Because only then will you stop cutting deals with pagan power brokers to insure your future. Your future is in God's hands!"

● ● ●

It is human nature to look for help when our backs are up against the wall. When the bills are past due, when schoolwork is stacking up, and when the business deal falls through, we look for alternative options. Avoiding those pressures is not an option. They are a part of life. Whether pressures will come is not an option, but where we go for ultimate help is. It is just too easy to run to Assyria, instead of God, with our problems.

Assyria seems more tangible, more immediate, more convincing. But God says to us what he said to Ahaz: "Ask me for a sign! Ask me for a sign to prove to you that I have the power to do the impossible. Make the request as difficult as you want. Nothing is too hard for me!"⁴

This is God's offer. But Ahaz said, "No, I will not put the Lord to the test. Israel and Syria are too big, and we're too puny. Against those kinds of odds we need something a lot more tangible than you, God. We need Assyria!"

But God will not be deterred. God knows that appealing to Assyria would mean disaster for Judah, and God will not let Judah go without a fight! And so God sends yet another message through Isaiah: "Trust me, Ahaz! Don't give in to this pressure. If you don't have the courage to choose a sign, then I *will* choose the sign. And here's the sign: a virgin shall conceive a child! She will give birth to a son and will call him Immanuel—God is with us. And before that child is even weaned from his mother's breast, the threat of Syria and Israel will be gone. You can trust me, Ahaz! No matter how great the odds stacked against you, if you put your faith in me, you will surely stand!" (Isa. 7:13-16, author's paraphrase).

When you really think about it, it must have seemed like a ridiculous promise to Ahaz. Ahaz was hanging from a branch looking into a very deep chasm. Ahaz didn't need a defenseless baby—he needed a powerful army!

Armies are what change destinies! Armies are what win victories! Armies change the world!

Don't they?

Empires, Wall Street, Main Street, the Dow Jones, data analytics, new technologies and innovations—these are the game changers.

Right? We would all like a little more assurance than a baby. Even a baby whose name is God among Us.

But as we hang from our branch, we discover that there really isn't anyone else up there.

● ● ●

When I interviewed at my second church, one of the first things I noticed was a golden shovel in the main foyer. On closer inspection, I discovered it was just a spray-painted shovel from Ace Hardware in a glass case.

I asked, "What's the shovel for?"

Someone said, "It's a *sign* to remind us that God has further plans for us."

I thought, *That takes a lot of faith.*

The church asked me to come as their pastor. I accepted.

A few months later, we began to outgrow our usable space. However, building anything more than we already had didn't seem possible at the time. We had a vision, but we didn't have the resources to fulfill it.[5]

One year later, we launched a building program. It was quite a project. It seemed like a giant to us. For one thing, we were not a congregation of wealthy folks. Most were very committed to the ministry, but not many were people of means. Additionally, the economy was faltering, the stock market was tanking, and people began losing their jobs. That was August 2001. One month later, 9/11 changed everything.

Our church leaders and pastoral staff discussed pulling the plug on the capital campaign or at least postponing it until things began to calm down. But none of us felt clear to do that. So we decided to forge ahead.

Naysayers were plentiful. I would tell people outside the church what we were attempting to do, and they would say, "That's great! What's your financial goal?" I would tell them, and they would look at me as though I had just lost a loved one. They would say, "Oh, my. Good luck with that."

Others offered advice. They would say, "Ordinarily this is what you can expect on a project like this: You first have to take into account your congregation's size and economic level—not to mention that you have a church with many young families, who, as everybody knows, don't usually give. Then when you add your missions giving on top of that, you'll find that you are really over-reaching."

I listened to the cynics and advisers. They all had valid arguments. We stayed the course and continued to pray.

The Wednesday night before our Pledge Sunday was designated as the time for our advanced commitment leaders to submit their faith goal amounts. The advanced commitments began trickling in, and for the first time I began to seriously wonder if we were going to reach our goal. We had been informed by some capital campaign gurus that for us to reach our financial goal a certain number of advanced gifts of a specified amount had to come in. We were far from both.

I went home that night more than a little discouraged. It felt as though we had an army advancing on us that we could not defeat. I had a wrestling match with God that night. I prayed, "God, I need your help. My faith is not very strong at the moment. I have to be able to stand up in front of our congregation on Sunday morning and ask them to make sacrificial pledges. I need to know that I'm not going in alone. I need a *sign* that you are with us."

God seemed to impress on me, "David, there's no need to panic. I am in control. Trust me. I am bigger than this giant."

And so I did. I left it in God's hands.

I had several appointments the next morning, and I finally arrived at the church office around ten. There was a pledge card sitting on my desk. I opened it up, and there was a faith commitment from one of our leadership families. It was a pledge for one hundred thousand dollars. I knew it was a significant sacrifice. I also knew it was a sign from God that he was with us.

Ten minutes later another person dropped by his commitment card. His family was new to the church. It was an equally sacrificial pledge of eighty-five thousand dollars. After a brief conversation together, he left. I began to cry like a baby. I got down on my knees and thanked God for his faithfulness to show me a sign.

Within a few hours more pledges came in that nearly doubled the amount from Wednesday night. It was God's way of saying, "What seems impossible to you is small potatoes for me. Trust me. The Sovereign Lord says so!"

We did not reach our pledge goal—we surpassed it! And when the amount was totaled, we all knew it wasn't because of our might, it wasn't because of our power, but it was because God was with us. God gave us the faith to believe that he would provide what we could never accomplish with our own strength or resources.

● ● ●

Nearly three thousand years ago, the king of Judah was hanging from a branch asking, "Is anybody else up there? Some Assyrians, maybe?"

Ahaz made a decision that was the most sensible to him at the time. It was reasonable, serviceable, and rational. It was faithless! He ignored God's promise to help because he couldn't trust the sign. The security of a baby was not enough, and he made a treaty with Assyria. That decision cost Judah dearly.

I want to grab Ahaz by the shirt and demand an answer: "What were you thinking? Why couldn't you trust God's promise?"

I want to do this until I remember that I have even less of an excuse for not trusting God's promise, because I live *after* Christmas. We all do. And with eyes of faith we see a hand stretched down to rescue us—Immanuel's[6] hand. Is a baby enough when we would prefer an army? Only if the baby is God among Us.

The angels announced to the shepherds at Christ's birth, "Glory to God in highest heaven, and peace on earth to those with whom God is pleased" (Luke 2:14, NLT). It is worth noting that there is "peace on earth" because Christ has come, but it also appears that this peace is for those who trust and follow him.

You will never have that peace if your definitive trust is in anyone or anything other than Christ, who is God among Us. There are a lot of people who believe in God but who don't have the peace God promises, because they are not completely trusting God to provide.

• • •

Some of you are hanging from a branch for dear life. God is saying, "Let me give you a sign."

Your first reaction might be to ask, "Is anybody else up there?"

Resist the temptation to hang on. Let go and reach out. The Sovereign Lord says so.

NOTES

Chapter 1

1. Mark Twain, "The American Vandal Abroad," in *Mark Twain's Speeches*, ed. Albert Bigelow Paine (New York: Harper and Brothers, 1923; repr., University of Virginia Library, 1996–2012), 21-30, http://twain.lib.virginia.edu/innocent/vandtext.html.

2. Leo Buscaglia was a teacher at University of Southern California and had the nickname Dr. Love. At one time he had five of his books on the *New York Times* Best Sellers list simultaneously.

3. Leo Buscaglia, *Papa, My Father: A Celebration of Dads* (New York: Fawcett Columbine, 1992), 17-19.

4. If you think about it, the very fact there is fighting today in the Gaza Strip is because four thousand years ago there were *two* brothers.

5. David M. Varner, *Sunday Funnies to Tickle the Soul* (Maitland, FL: Xulon Press, 2010), 35.

6. *Imago Dei* is a Latin term that means "image of God." Apparently, our inherent value as human beings is completely independent of our usefulness or performance.

7. God gave them another son much later named Seth. Seth means "granted."

8. This is why Wesley was so amped up about small groups focused on responsible grace. This is also why Wesleyan-Holiness folks are so adamant about accountable relationships.

Chapter 2

1. *Thinkexist.com*, s.v. "C. S. Lewis quotes," accessed January 10, 2013, http://thinkexist.com/quotation/miracles_are_a_retelling_in_small_letters_of_the/202038.html.

2. In the picture I saw of them, she looked tired and he was smiling.

3. Even though polygamy was a common custom in ancient society, even a quick overview of the Hebrew Scriptures would suggest that the practice almost always is disruptive and causes strife within the family units involved.

4. Sarah does not even bother to call Hagar and Ishmael by their names. They are merely "that slave woman and her son."

5. One of my favorite promises in Scripture is the Rom. 8:26 reminder that when we don't know what to pray for, the Spirit intercedes on our behalf with groans that words cannot express.

6. *Creatio ex nihilo* is a Latin phrase that means "creation out of nothing."

7. Along with v. 9, this verse is the scriptural basis for Bruce Wilkinson's *The Prayer of Jabez: Breaking Through to the Blessed Life* (Colorado Springs: Multnomah Books, 2000).

Chapter 3

1. Sufjan Stevens, "Abraham," *Seven Swans*, Sounds Familyre SF013, 2004, compact disc. For complete lyrics, see http://www.stlyrics.com/songs/s /sufjanstevens25453/abraham1097534.html.

2. "Flat out" is an Oklahoma expression used only on special occasions to underscore bluntness and to state the obvious: "That Adrian Peterson can flat out run the football."

3. The Hebrew word for Isaac, *Yitskhaq*, means "he laughs."

4. I will never forget the first time I heard my friend Jeff Crosno tell his version of this story. It makes me smile even today.

5. *Lekh-Lekha* is the Hebrew word "Go!" or "Leave!"

6. Moriah is where many scholars believe the Temple Mount in Jerusalem is today.

7. Fourth-century theologian Jerome suggests that the age of weaning for Hebrew children could have been as late as twelve years old.

8. Talmud scholars estimate that Isaac was thirty-seven years old at the time of this event.

9. The Hebrew language here is emphatic. If you were Isaac, you would want God to shout!

10. I think I heard a preacher say this phrase once. I don't remember who said it, but I've never forgotten the impact it made on me.

Chapter 4

1. *Brainy Quote*, s.v. "Impatience Quotes," accessed January 14, 2013, http://www.brainyquote.com/quotes/keywords/impatience.html.

2. Esau literally means "hairy." Edom, another name Esau was called, means "red."

3. Apparently, baby name books were not available to parents in Bible times.

4. The whole dress-up scheme in Gen. 27 was about trying to secure his father's blessing.

5. Robert Alter, *Genesis: Translation and Commentary* (New York: W. W. Norton and Company, 1996), 129.

6. Ibid.

7. Ibid.

8. Frederick Buechner, *The Magnificent Defeat* (1966; repr., New York: HarperCollins Publishers, 1985), 14. One of my favorite books on the Jacob

story is Buechner's *The Son of Laughter.* Once I started reading it, I couldn't put it down.

Chapter 5

1. *Brainy Quote*, s.v. "Righteousness Quotes," accessed January 14, 2013, http://www.brainyquote.com/quotes/keywords/righteousness_2.html.

2. You know you're a model prisoner when you are given the keys to the jail.

3. Apparently there is still good money to be made in dream interpretation today. I Googled "dream interpretation" and found a website called whispy .com. The advertisement read, "Analysis Special of the Week. Will interpret your dreams in 10 minutes for $1.99."

4. Walter Brueggemann, *Genesis*, Interpretation: A Bible Commentary for Teaching and Preaching (Louisville, KY: John Knox Press, 1982), 293, italics in the original.

5. This is a paraphrase of something I heard Dr. Tim Keller say in a sermon on God's providence.

6. If you're interested in the math, at the time I am writing this chapter, the United States of America is 236 years old.

7. A gold chain was the highest distinction a king could bestow on a citizen.

8. This is my paraphrase and addition to a quote I read somewhere from David Starr Jordan, the founding president of Stanford.

9. Julius Caesar "J. C." Watts Jr. said these insightful words to me in a personal conversation. J. C. was a United States congressman. He also played quarterback for my favorite college football team.

Chapter 6

1. *oChristian Christian Quotes*, s.v. "Leonard Ravenhill Quotes," accessed January 16, 2013, http://christian-quotes.ochristian.com/Leonard-Ravenhill -Quotes/page-4.shtml.

2. Blaise Pascal, "Memorial" (1654), Christian Classics Ethereal Library, accessed January 16, 2013, http://www.ccel.org/ccel/pascal/memorial.txt.

3. Jim Cymbala wrote a very popular book about this called *Fresh Wind, Fresh Fire* (Grand Rapids: Zondervan, 1997).

4. The Hebrew word for "tabernacle" is *mishkan*. It can also mean "tent" or "hut," but it often means far more than that. *Mishkan* is also related to the Hebrew word meaning "to dwell," "to rest," or "to live in," referring to the *shekinah* glory of God that dwelled or rested wherever or whenever the presence of God inhabited a place or person.

5. John Newton is also known for writing the fairly popular hymn "Amazing Grace."

Chapter 7

1. *ThinkExist.com*, s.v. "Søren Kierkegaard quotes," accessed January 16, 2013, http://thinkexist.com/quotation/life_can_only_be_understood_back wards-but_it_must/12046.html.

2. This is from the Mishneh Torah, Sefer Ahavah, Tefilah and Birkat Kohanim, Chapter 7, Halacha 6 (emphasis added). A version of this blessing may be found at http://www.chabad.org/library/article_cdo/aid/920169/jewish /Chapter-Seven.htm.

3. Because Tyre and Sidon were famous Canaanite cities, and centers of great commercial activity, the name Canaanite came to signify a "trader" or "merchant." Some scholars now maintain that the Canaanite reputation for cruelty may be trumped up from Ugaritic myths from the north.

4. There is currently a scholarly debate going on about the veracity of sacred prostitution, particularly in ancient Israel. In some instances of Scripture, *qedeshah* and *zonah* appear to be interchangeable.

5. *Wikipedia,* s.v. "Rahab," accessed March 11, 2013, http://en.wikipedia.org /wiki/Rahab.

6. H. Orton Wiley, *The Epistle to the Hebrews,* rev. ed. (Kansas City: Beacon Hill Press of Kansas City, 1984), 334.

7. Check out the genealogy of Jesus in Matt. 1. Rahab's name is there, along with four other women with checkered pasts. Even Mary, Jesus' mother, had to live with rumors of his "illegitimate" birth.

8. I got this concept from a very good pastor named Craig Groeschel.

Chapter 8

1. *BrainyQuote*, s.v. "Plato Quotes," accessed January 17, 2012, http:// www.brainyquote.com/quotes/authors/p/plato.html.

2. John Ortberg, "Big God/Little God," God Is Big Enough (sermon series, Menlo Park Presbyterian Church, Menlo Park, CA, October 27-28, 2007), 2, http://www.mppc.org/sites/default/files/transcripts/071028_jort berg.pdf. I heard John Ortberg preach this sermon at a conference. His profound way with words always amazes me.

3. Actually, I just made that part up about stuff between your toes, but the rest is true.

4. This might be a good time to go write that quote down in your journal.

5. Go ahead. Write it down.

6. Dale Ralph Davis, *Judges: Such a Great Salvation,* Focus on the Bible (2003; repr., Ross-shire, Scotland: Christian Focus Publications, 2007), chap. 9.

7. Douglas Stuart, quoted in Ortberg, "Big God/Little God," 35. Douglas Stuart teaches at Gordon Conwell Seminary, is proficient in fourteen languages, and has written extensively on the Old Testament. One of his books,

cowritten with Gordon Fee, is called *How to Read the Bible for All Its Worth.* I highly recommend it.

8. Ortberg, "Big God/Little God," 7. This is a quote from the same sermon I referred to in endnote 2.

9. Some examples include Gen. 26:24; Deut. 31:6; Josh. 8:1; Luke 1:30; and Rev. 1:17.

Chapter 9

1. *Goodreads*, s.v. "Ralph Waldo Emerson," accessed January 18, 2013, http://www.goodreads.com/author/quotes/12080.Ralph_Waldo_Emerson ?page=5.

2. Throughout Scripture God seems to delight in helping barren people who have run out of options.

3. The phrase "went down" is both a geographical and a spiritual inference.

4. There is that phrase again.

5. Nazirite vow number three will be broken when he sleeps with Delilah and she cuts his hair.

6. Gentlemen, if you're having a spat with your wife, there's nothing that says "I love you" like a young goat.

Chapter 10

1. Michael Gungor, "Beautiful Things," *Beautiful Things*, Brash Music BRH00562, 2010, compact disc. For complete lyrics, http://www.metrolyrics .com/beautiful-things-lyrics-gungor.html.

2. I am a Eugene Peterson fan. One of my favorite books of his is called *Leap Over a Wall: Earthy Spirituality for Everyday Christians* (New York: Harper-Collins, 1997). This consists of his reflections on the life of David. Many of my ideas in this chapter were formed from reading his book.

3. Jude v. 24 is a verse about the keeping grace of God that can protect us from falling. The verses prior are about helping protect others from falling.

4. I give credit to Eugene Peterson for helping me to see the power of beauty as an icon through which we see God more clearly.

5. Peterson, *Leap Over a Wall*, 81.

6. One of my favorite songs right now about the power of God to transform human lives is Michael Gungor's "Beautiful Things." One of the verses says, "All around, / Hope is springing up from this old ground. / Out of chaos life is being found in You" (*Beautiful Things*, Brash Music BRH00562, 2010).

Chapter 11

1. Thomas Keating, *Invitation to Love: The Way of Christian Contemplation* (New York: Continuum International Publishing Group, 2006), 90.

2. Scott Daniels is a Nazarene pastor in Southern California who inspires me to want to be a better preacher.

3. This entire story can be found in 1 Kings 18. It is worth the time to reread it.

4. Reading Eugene Peterson's paraphrase of this in *The Message* makes me smile.

5. The gospel writer Mark uses a more forceful term than "led." He says the Spirit "drove" Jesus into the wilderness (Mark 1:12, NKJV).

6. Henri Nouwen, *The Way of the Heart: The Spirituality of the Desert Fathers and Mothers* (New York: HarperCollins Publishers, 1981), 25. Nouwen's words and life stretch my thinking.

Chapter 12

1. *Goodreads*, s.v. "C. S. Lewis," accessed January 24, 2013, http://www.goodreads.com/author/quotes/1069006.C_S_Lewis?page=6.

2. The Law was the first five books of the Bible. Also called the Torah, Genesis through Deuteronomy, these books were probably more or less in the same form as we have them today.

3. Standing is a sign of reverence and respect. When I am preaching, I often ask the congregation to stand during the reading of God's Word.

4. Also known as the Old Testament.

5. I have personally seen similar stone jars in the Middle East, and I can tell you that they are quite large.

6. Since I am a minister in good standing with the Church of the Nazarene, I do not imbibe in wine drinking. Therefore, I have purposefully excised the source of this analysis from my mind.

7. I am thoroughly enjoying creating at least half of these endnotes with tongue-firmly-in-cheek. See endnote 6 for reference.

8. This is my very loose paraphrase of Matt. 9:15; Mark 2:19; and Luke 5:34. What Jesus' detractors didn't seem to grasp is that not only did Jesus' disciples practice fasting, but also Jesus assumed they would. In his Sermon on the Mount Jesus said, "When you fast . . ." (Matt. 6:16-18).

9. How do you slander someone who doesn't do things the way you think he or she should? Pick a spiritual topic (like fasting or repentance) and label him or her the opposite (glutton or drunkard). See Matt. 11:19 and Luke 7:34.

10. I am laughing right now as I write this.

11. Mark Buchanan, *Your God Is Too Safe* (Sisters, OR: Multnomah Publishers, 2001), 241.

12. Ibid., 242.

13. Carl Bangs has written an excellent biography of Bresee's life titled *Phineas F. Bresee: His Life in Methodism, the Holiness Movement, and the Church of the Nazarene* (Kansas City: Beacon Hill Press of Kansas City, 1995). I highly recommend it.

Chapter 13

1. *QuotationsBook*, s.v. "Boom, Corrie Ten," accessed January 22, 2013, http://quotationsbook.com/quote/16484/.

2. This happened two hundred years before Isaiah the prophet was born.

3. If Isaiah's sense of direction was anything like mine, God would have to be specific!

4. It always surprises me when God invites us to test his power. Evidently, God knows that sometimes our faith needs something tangible to hang on to.

5. While it's true that without a vision the people perish, it is also true that without resources the vision perishes.

6. The name Immanuel means "God with us."

The New Testament is filled with stories of people with all kinds of flaws and imperfections. The astounding thing is what happens when God changes their lives.

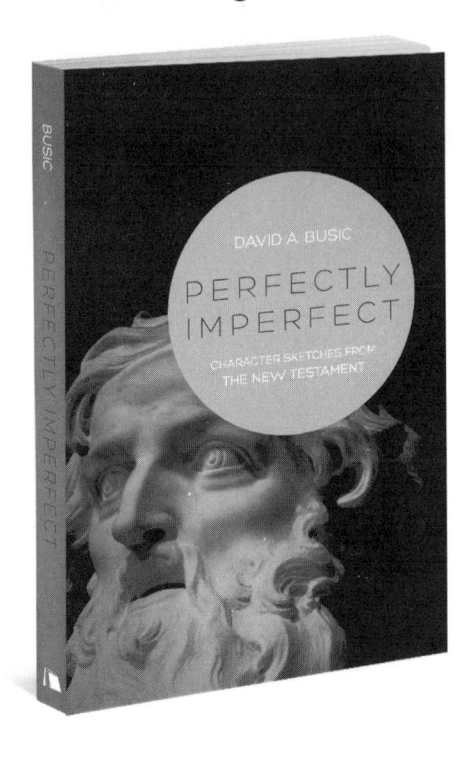

Perfectly Imperfect is about people whose true-to-life stories are found in the New Testament. They are like us in many ways— confused, tempted, and often afraid. They are flawed, real people, but then God enters their lives, and everything changes. In these sometimes tragic and broken lives, we get a glimpse of how God renews us and remakes us into people who are perfectly imperfect.

Available Spring 2014

BEACON HILL PRESS
OF KANSAS CITY

Perfectly Imperfect
ISBN: 978-0-8341-3096-8

Available online at BeaconHillBooks.com